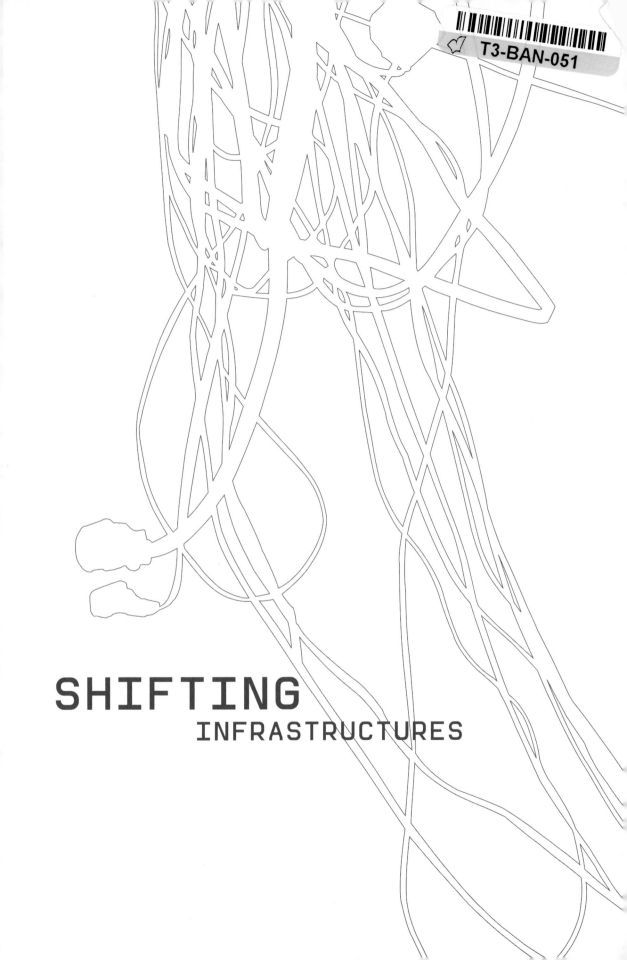

SHIFTING
INFRASTRUCTURES

306090   06

Patricia Acevedo-Riker
Martha Merzig
John Riker
Jeremi Sudol
306090 06 > Editors

306090, Inc.

Alexander F. Briseño
Jonathan D. Solomon
Series Editors and Publishers

Emily A. Abruzzo
Senior Editor

Andrew Yang
Special Projects Editor

Cover
Oh, So and So
www.ohsoandso.com

Cable Line-Art
www.telephonemusic.net

Thanks to
Alan Balfour, Dean
        Rensselaer Polytechnic Institute
        School of Architecture
Mark Owens, David Reinfurt, Stewart Smith
        www.o-r-g.com
David Riebe
Craig Somers

306090 is an independent architectural journal published and distributed semi-annually. 306090 seeks to publish diverse, inquisitive projects by students and young professionals that have not been published elsewhere.

Opinions expressed in 306090 are the author's alone and do not necessarily reflect those of the editors.

Distributed by:
        Princeton Architectural Press
        37 East Seventh Street
        New York, New York 10003
        1.800.722.6657

Contact publisher for Library of Congress Cataloging-in-Publication Data

www.306090.org   info@306090.org

306090, Inc. is a non-profit institution registered in the states of New York and New Jersey. Your donations are tax deductible. For more information on how to contribute or to submit work please contact us at: info@306090.org or visit our Web site. For ordering information contact the Princeton Architectural Press at orders@papress.org

ISBN 1-56898-475-8

306090, Inc.
350 Canal Street
Box 2092
New York, NY 10013-0875

Increasingly, our territorial and occupational processes are negotiated vis-à-vis mobile communication methods and information technologies. Communication networks and systems of data and material distribution — newscasts, fashion trends, product shipping, peer-to-peer file sharing software — create their own unique infrastructures and inform existing exchange structures. Newscasts require and affect events reported; they also require and affect the physical communications hardware over which they are broadcast. New analytical methods reveal thresholds, transitions, redundancies and discontinuities embedded in this dynamic of infrastructural exchange, which suggest processes to tactically unleash immanent manifestations of matter and information.

    306090 06 > SHIFTING INFRASTRUCTURES will examine the current technological infiltration into civic and social realms, where physical and cultural infrastructures are redefining themselves as shifting, modulating entities across diverse spatial and temporal scales.

CONTENTS

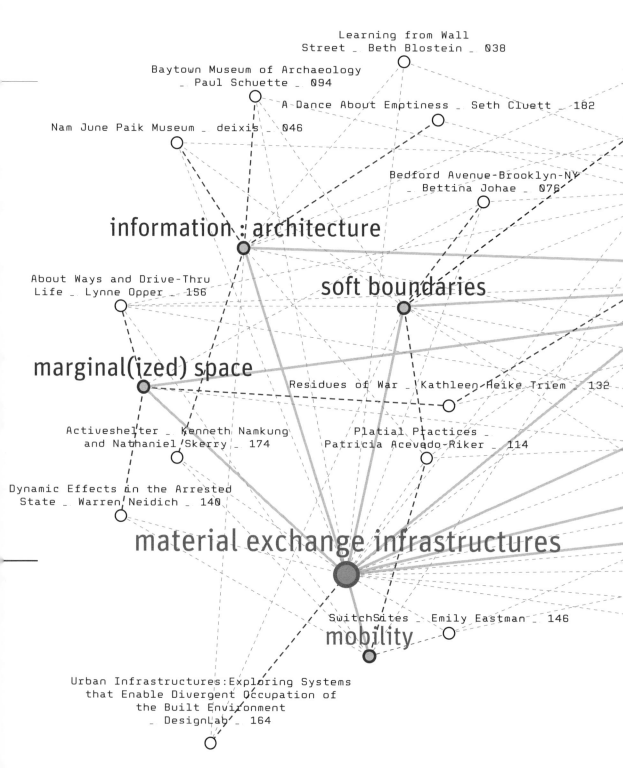

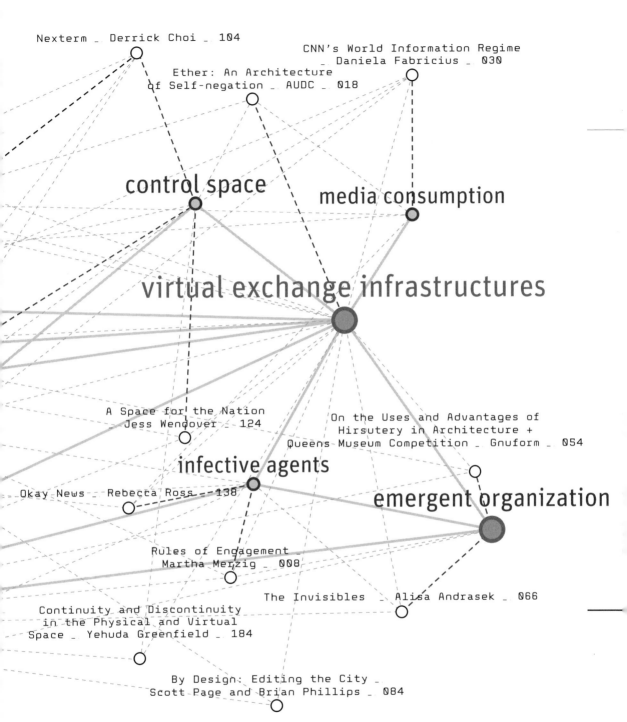

Nexterm _ Derrick Choi _ 104

CNN's World Information Regime
_ Daniela Fabricius _ 030

Ether: An Architecture
of Self-negation _ AUDC _ 018

control space

media consumption

virtual exchange infrastructures

A Space for the Nation
_ Jess Wendover _ 124

On the Uses and Advantages of
Hirsutery in Architecture +
Queens Museum Competition _ Gnuform _ 054

infective agents

Okay News _ Rebecca Ross _ 138

emergent organization

Rules of Engagement _
Martha Menzig _ 008

The Invisibles _ Alisa Andrasek _ 066

Continuity and Discontinuity
in the Physical and Virtual
Space _ Yehuda Greenfield _ 184

By Design: Editing the City _
Scott Page and Brian Phillips _ 084

SHIFTING INFRASTRUCTURES

Exchange Structures

Infrastructure, as defined in Webster's dictionary, is an "underlying foundation or basic framework — as of a system or organization."[1] Although traditionally thought of as large-scale, engineered public works, *infrastructures* are all — at least on some level — data-structures, mediating exchange processes. Language can be considered an infrastructure: the conventions of the signs, sounds, gestures and marks we use allow us to communicate based on learned and understood meanings.[2] Most alphabets, however, require shifts and diacritics[3] to distinguish multiple meanings and add layers of complexity.

shift — *noun* : **V. 14. d.** a phonetic change **19.** a change from one set of characters to another[4]

di·a·crit·ic — a mark near or through an orthographic or phonetic character or combination of characters indicating a phonetic value different from that given the unmarked or otherwise marked element[5]

Master Tacticians

Starting out with only a handful of basic, self-taught gestures, a group of deaf Nicaraguan children collectively constructed an entirely new language. In less than two and a half decades, Nicaraguan Sign Language has flourished, with virtually no external instruction or guidance. The teachers tasked with enabling the children to communicate adopted a flawed pedagogy, and were therefore unable to leverage any sort of effect on the children's improvised language. This allowed the children freedom to build their own linguistic structure with unique grammar and syntax. As such, the new language does not resemble Spanish at all.

Upon arriving in Nicaragua in the mid 1980s, Judy Kegl, an American sign-language expert, according to an article in the *New York Times*, visited two schools for the deaf — first Villa Libertad, a vocational school and later San Judas, a primary school.

It was noticeable at once that the younger children used signs in a more nuanced way than the older students. For example, the teen-age pidgin signers at Villa Libertad had a basic gesture for *speak* — opening and closing four fingers and a thumb in front of the mouth. The younger children used the same sign, but modulated it, opening their fingers at the position of the speaker and closing them at the position of the addressee. To Kegl, this apparently small difference had enormous implications. "This was verb agreement," she says, "and they were all using it fluently."[6]

tac·ti·cal — **2. a.** of or relating to tactics: as (1) : of or relating to small-scale actions serving a larger purpose[7]

tac·tic — *noun* : **1.** a device for accomplishing an end[8]

-tac·tic — *adjective combining form* : **2.** showing orientation or movement directed by a — specified — force or agent[9]

shift — *noun* : **I. 1. a.** a movement to do something, a beginning **III. 3. a.** an expedient, an ingenious device for effecting some purpose[10]

These observations serve as evidence to the evolution of an entwined, complex structure. In mastering the language of their elder peers, the students of San Judas initiated tactical shifts in their communication with each other, causing the language to blossom from its modest beginnings in only a handful of years. Still communicating with the same basic elements as the older students, the younger students intuitively employed these apparently small agents, thus revealing profound new meanings within the same linguistic structure.

In more than one sense the children of San Judas can be considered master tacticians — but this is not to say that the ends are apparent from within the exchange structure. The end — or larger purpose — only reveals itself in the actualization. "The actualization of the virtual . . . always takes place by difference, divergence or differentiation."[13]

tac·ti·cian — one versed in tactics[11]

tac·tics — *noun plural but singular or plural in construction* : **1. b.** the art or skill of employing available means to accomplish an end **2.** a system or mode of procedure **3.** the study of the grammatical relations within a language including morphology and syntax[12]

Our existing and emerging physical and data-based infrastructures are rife with opportunities for tactical engagement — to initiate tactical shifts. Mobile populations and fluctuating economies will apply steady pressure to our infrastructures — careful analysis will indicate where to direct these shifts.

Shift, as a verb, *to* "exchange for or replace by another,"[14] is not to be ignored, but when speaking of vast meshworks, such as communication networks and systems of data and material distribution, it is not necessarily productive or realistic to enact sweeping reform — from the top, down. Through the deployment of specified agents of diacritical shift at appropriate — and specific — scales and locations, new meaning(s) can be revealed within a greater infrastructural and cultural context.

NOTES

1. *Merriam-Webster Online Dictionary*, <http://www.m-w.com>, 2004
2. Ibid, Merriam-Webster Online
3. Hays, D., *Introduction to Computational Linguistics*. New York, American Elsevier, 1967.
4. *Oxford English Dictionary Online*, <http://www.oed.com>, 2004.
5. *Merriam-Webster Online Dictionary*, <http://www.m-w.com> 2004
6. Osborne, Lawrence, "A Linguistic Big Bang," *The New York Times*, October 24, 1999.
7. *Merriam-Webster Online Dictionary*, <http://www.m-w.com>, 2004.
8. Ibid, Merriam-Webster Online
9. Ibid, Merriam-Webster Online
10. *Oxford English Dictionary Online*, <http://www.oed.com>, 2004.
11. *Merriam-Webster Online Dictionary*, <http://www.m-w.com>, 2004.
12. Ibid.
13. Deleuze, Gilles, *Difference and Repetition*, Columbia University Press, New York, 1994
14. *Merriam-Webster Online Dictionary*, <http://www.m-w.com>, 2004.

Fold diagram by Oh, So and So, and inspired by the work of Rene Thom.

Martha Merzig

The Internet

Real understanding of the Internet and its effects can only take place decades from now. It is too early in the life or development of the World Wide Web to be certain of its meaning. Despite uncertainties about its future, its short life has nevertheless been an eventful one. It has made millionaires and broken physical boundaries in unexpected ways. It has allowed for new modes of communication and enhanced existing ones. New opportunities and methods of commerce have been developed.

Faking It: Knowledge is Power

Andy Kessler, a venture capitalist, keeps a list in his pocket. This list contains conflicts he has observed between industry outsiders and insiders. Part of it reads:

> EBay trader vs. newspaper publisher
> home schooling vs. public schools
> hacker vs. corporate security
> Carsdirect.com vs. car dealership
> Linux vs. Microsoft
> Exodus Data Housing Center vs. the Pentagon
> email spammer vs. Madison Ave. Creative Director[1]

Life online seems to allow do-it-yourselfers as much legitimacy as those with formal training. Availability of information is up-ending the established social hierarchy of in- and outsider. Information allows 15 year olds to have equal power and share in a company as any 40 year old. It allows those with no formal training to practice their expertise with as much legitimacy as someone with a formal education. Those whose professions were, and continue to be, based largely on knowledge and intellectual property — attorneys, stock brokers, doctors, record executives — are now in danger of losing their jobs to self-educated *novices*. Those who once were outsiders now have all — or most — of the same information available to them as their professional counterparts.

Underneath the Global Network

Refugee peoples and lands are growing in number. Displaced and migrant peoples, itinerants and ethnic groups without territory, these peoples remain politically and economically unrepresented within the global community — except within the marketing strategies of international relief organizations.

"(N)ational borders all over the world (have) become ever less permeable which may be explained by the easy availability of surveillance electronics and passive war machinery, especially mines. Borders can be projected at whim with a minimum of effort. On the other hand, ethnic, national, and geographical zones of tolerance fall victim to the transportation and information revolution/explosion. . . The officially acknowledged 23 million refugees of an ever-growing refugee population — unofficially estimated at 50 million — is scattered all over the world, parked in UN camps. By now, the number of unregistered displaced persons worldwide has reached one percent of the world population. . .

"Presently, refugees are nearly always regarded as an economic and social burden. . . Recognized as (such) by the UN — and several international conventions — they are kept alive in camps, prisoners of international charity with their status established and confirmed."[2] Caught between borders and between cultures, these refugees must sustain themselves within a political and economic no-man's-land.

Likewise, bypassed lands and communities and places with weak or absent connection to urban centers are caught between, and develop against, borders. They are the result of economic oddities: air force bases, oil wells, traffic flow diverted by highways and interstates, abandoned major rail lines, truck stops. They are the residue of systems deployed as industrial and/or tactical operators.

Technology and Exclusion

Recently, personal and social communication has begun to shift from primarily storytelling modes to more data-based and anonymous modes of exchange. Personal communication has shifted from slow, continuous, fluid, idea-laden discourse to broken, collage-like digital information exchange. This shift of modes brings with it a shift of dialogue structures: Dialogue moves from the oral — modes in which information is evolutionary, ephemeral, and dependant upon time and place — to the digital — modes in which information is condensed, encoded, and preserved. Those who are unfulfilled by or uninterested in this new mode of communication become increasingly alienated.

This condition, however, seems to be a symptom of a larger situation. The changes that are gradually taking place in our communication methods are also happening in our marketplace. Those whose needs do not easily fit into consumer groups or are largely unreachable — or seem to be unaffected — by mass marketing often go unrecognized as members of society. The technologically inept are also becoming less able participants.

Cold, Hard Cash

Right now, the success of technology requires capital, and lots of it. Technology is expensive to research, produce and market. New, smaller, and ever faster gadgets are being showered upon consumers, from cell phones, digital cameras and mp3 players, to electronic date books, GPS systems, laptops, and on and on. Each plaything requires both time and money to operate, maintain, upgrade, and align with all of the gadgets working in tandem with it. Access to these objects is for the most part a middle- and upper-class-only privilege. It is imperative that the underprivileged also have access to parts of this technological revolution, else the gap between rich and poor will widen even more. Public access to the internet and communication networks must happen with the same breadth and ease of access as public restrooms and public parks. Developing countries and the underprivileged must be able to participate fully in the evolving global network, and so must have access to this communications medium.

Energy, Means, Materials

Our energy and economic resources are limited. The Internet depends largely upon electricity and the infrastructure that supports energy production and distribution. Even in this country, what we once thought were boundless energy sources are beginning to show signs of weakness. The Internet — in this country, at least — is dependent upon an infrastructure that is costly to install and/or modify. In developing countries in which there are no means or no municipal or federal support for installation of internet-ready lines, alternate means must be found. Cell phones abound in Eastern Europe, for example, because the infrastructures to adequately support telephone land lines are unavailable and digital wireless technology exists that is more reliable and less expensive. We must seek new ways of powering and connecting ourselves to one another that are less taxing to our energy stores and do not require the complex infrastructure that we in the United States take for granted.

Networks, Geographies, Infrastructures
Physical/Informational Phenomena

There exist networks, both physical and informational, that affect and are affected by the data that flows along them. They are tied to the social, cultural, and physical landscapes within which they operate. These networks, be they migration routes, the ebb and flow of tourists at a theme park, the intensities of information transmittal over fiberoptic cables, simultaneously operate across both the virtual and the physical.

Physical/Digital Infrastructure

The internet, a highly fluid information network in terms of the infinite number of possible connections between individual and groups of users, is nevertheless strongly related to the physical geographies and infrastructures within which it operates. Although these connections are not determined exclusively by physical phenomena, a clear relationship exists between the two. Also, the way in which constituent points are networked is incredibly important; it will either ensure or frustrate the way in which users communicate and groups are reached.

Data Hacking: Defacers

There exist people groups who operate underneath global informational networks. Hackers and web defacers like the Brazilian Silver Lords organization operate outside the corporate body, bypassing rules and making war against information hoarders. Linux is popular not only because it can be functionally more powerful than a Windows operating system, but because it bares all the information and encoding that Windows buries.

Jonathan Lebed, a 15-year-old New Jersey boy, inflated the price of stocks by posting numerous messages to a Yahoo.com message board. He made over $800,000 in after-school trading.[3]

Marcus Arnold, also fifteen, was ranked the #1 legal expert on the AskMe.com Web site during the year 2000. Almost all of his legal knowledge came

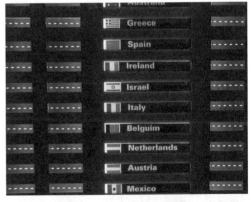

from legal Web sites and a steady diet of police and court television shows.[4]

These boys are hackers as much as the Silver Lords: they creatively overcome rules and operate underneath global informational networks. On the internet, these boys are indistinguishable from traditionally educated sources.

Political Hacking: Sealand

Hacking does not require a computer, but there is something about the digital that encourages it like nothing else. Sealand, a country whose only land is an abandoned British WWII sea base, exists in a political no-man's-land. It and its inhabitants operate between and against traditional borders. Among the many unique border conditions operating in and around Sealand, one is particularly interesting: it is now home to HavenCo, a data haven, a completely anonymous information storage center. HavenCo's storage system is the informational version of a Swiss bank account: the company agrees to store digital information on highly secure servers without ever revealing your identity or regulating the content of the information stored there.

Political Hacking: Surveillance and Tracking

Technology is now available that uses photographs to produce and render, in real-time, 3D models of large-scale terrain. The U.S. Government used this technology when at war with Afghanistan to remotely monitor the progress and success of airborne missions in that country. This technology increases the possibility for surveillance — both foreign and domestic — resulting in less privacy and less anonymity. Increasingly, control over and access to surveillance technologies affords incredible power to those countries and governments that own them.

Migrant Flow and Exchange Fields

Certain regions act as infrastructural thresholds within large-scale network structures. They are points of entry for and major structural actors along fields of information exchange. The peoples and things that inhabit these routes are diverse and evolutionary. Exchange fields mediate the actual and the virtual and include almost any transaction and flow: agriculture, tourism, transportation, currency trajectory, social strata, immigration trends, gerrymandering, linguistics.

Exchange Infrastructures

SOCIAL STATUS— To market their newest game, Pox, Hasbro searched for *alpha pups*, the coolest boys, and gave them game units. The boys did the rest.[5]

MIGRANT POPULATIONS   MIGRANT FLOW SITES

San Diego / NORTH:
Surfers
Imperial/Mission/
Pacific Beaches
Freeways
Sports Arenas
Tijuana Tourist Districts

Tourists
Freeways
Hotels
Amusement Parks
Sports Arenas
Beaches
Tijuana Tourist Districts

Navy Personnel
Beaches
Sports Arenas
Navy Bases
Harbor Areas
Tijuana Tourist Districts

BORDER CROSSING/SAN YSIDRO

Tijuana / SOUTH:
Truckers
Freight Transfer Sites
Freeways
Maquiladoras
Southern Factories

Taxi Drivers
Tourist Districts
Garages
Local Neigborhoods

Maquiladora Workers
Bus Shuttles/Stops
Ciudad Industrial
Local Neigborhoods

Street Vendors
Tourist Districts
Maquiladora Areas

NEWARK/JERSEY CITY/HOBOKEN

Exchange Field
Commuter Infrastructure

Exchange Interfaces
Roadway Scale Changes
Train Stops
Rest Stops
Toll Gates

Theshold Colonies
Commuters
Service Workers
Bypassed Neighborhoods

ATLANTIC CITY: CAPITAL CONCENTRATION

Exchange Field
Currency
Entertainment
Service

Exchange Interfaces
Banks/ATMs
Hotels
Casino Floors
Boardwalk

Theshold Colonies
Casino Workers
Hotel Maids/Staff

SAN DIEGO: BORDERLAND

Exchange Field
Agriculture
Immigration

Exchange Interfaces
Baja Border/Fence Crossing
Crop Shipments
Field Work

Theshold Colonies
Illegal Immigrants
Migrant/Agricultural Labor
INS Border Patrol

LINGUISTIC INFECTION/EVOLUTION— Deaf Nicaraguan children, unable to attend school, developed their own sign language to communicate with each other and the outside world.[6]

CURRENCY TRAJECTORY— At Where'sGeorge.com, users can register and track the movement of small bills.

SEARCH AND RESCUE OPERATIONS— As emergency teams are deployed, new — but temporary — behaviors and alliances occur around the participant organizations and individuals.

INFORMATION TRAILS— Pheromone evaporation determines the frequency and order of food collection around ant colonies. After foraging randomly, the ants begin to raid the food sources that are closest. As those supplies dwindle, the concentration of pheromone along their trails decreases through evaporation. The ants will then exploit the farther source.

Virtual Defined

The virtual negotiates between the material and the immaterial, the scientific and the social, the quantifiable and the immeasurable.

The virtual, of course, is not equivalent to the digital. Neither can it be fully realized in the possible or the actual. John Rajchman describes the virtual as *multiple potential*. The virtual, he says, is "not an abstraction, a generality, or an a priori condition. It does not take us from the specific to the generic. It increases possibility in another way: it mobilizes as yet un-specifiable singularities, bringing them together in an indeterminate plan." He says that "the virtual lies in forces or potentials whose origins and outcomes cannot be specified independently of the open and necessarily incomplete series of their actualizations. . . To virtualize nature is . . . not to double it, but, on the contrary, to multiply it, complicate it, release other forms and paths in it."[7]

> The Virtual House . . . is the one whose arrangement or disposition allows for the greater number of singular points and the most complex connections among them . . . (The virtual is) so *smooth* that fixed qualities do not stick to it . . . It is free just because it is neither ideal nor impossible . . . It says *no* only to affirm new possibilities through a virtual construction that says *yes* as well as *and*.
> —John Rajchman[8]

Rajchman also believes that the virtual legitimizes the image — and/or object. When the possibilities for a thing are already laid out, when everything is clear — *i.e.* when that thing lacks potential to become something other or to operate differently; when it takes no part in the virtual — it seems counterfeit, hollow.

Virtual, Material, Temporal

The virtual, then, does not operate alone. It manifests itself in conjunction with the actual: it is tied to the actual in that the virtual necessarily engages with and becomes visible via the actual. Brian Massumi describes the virtual/actual — or, as stated by Massumi, the virtual/analog — relationship as thus:

An analog process is the continuous transformation of an impulse from one qualitatively different medium into another. Electricity into sound waves. Or heat into pain. Or light waves into vision. Or vision into imagination . . . Or of the outside as a coming in. Sensation is the analog processing by the body of impinging forces . . . Every possibility and potential, however calculated, retains an irrevocable residue of qualitative difference, to which it owes its distinctness. That residue or reserve . . . is virtuality, as enveloped in the given: the virtual in its empirical presentation.

He goes on to describe this relationship in terms of digital technologies: "(T)he digital is virtualized and potentialized only in its integrative circuiting with the analog (the material), in the way in which it is integrated into the analog or integrates the analog into itself."[5]

The information transmission described by Massumi of heat into pain, or light into vision, are actions taken over time. It is the transformation of material and the temporal through which the virtual reveals itself. It is through the multiplicity, the *yes, and,* of the material and its transformation that the virtual becomes perceptible.

The Complex, the Communicated, and the Controlled

At the 1991 SIGGRAPH conference, programmer Loren Carpenter conducted a 5,000 person game of Pong. In this experiment, each member of the audience holds a wand, green on one side, red on the other. Displaying the red side of the wand moves the paddle up, green moves the paddle down. Based on Ken Goldberg's algorithm for collaborative control, the program averages the number of red and green it sees and moves the paddle appropriately. Each wand equals just one vote. The audience split into two teams, each side controlling a paddle. What resulted was a "reasonably good

game of Pong."[9] After a few minutes of game play, the ball in play sped up. The crowd faltered, but then quickly compensated, playing better than before. Again the ball gained speed, again the crowd compensated and improved. Once the game of Pong ended, Carpenter tried other experiments on this crowd with their wands, having them make simple patterns and, later, having them successfully control a flight simulator.

Games like this are interesting because they reveal the potential of decentralized, networked groups: between the players emerges an intelligence. Each player in the group is responsive to all the others, modifying their behavior according to the behavior of the whole. Each red/green voter learned how to integrate themselves into the mob appropriately to achieve a certain task.

Like Carpenter's Pong players, network systems tend to be decentralized and dumb, containing redundant paths and possibilities. John Arquilla and David Ronfeldt, military analysts at the RAND Corporation, study the internal operation of terrorist organizations. They describe "developed" organizations in terms of their communication modes and methods.

The viability of groups such as these hinges on their adaptability and ability to communicate. Full-fledged *netwar actors*, like Al Queda and Hamas, utilize every resource and technology available to them: high- and low-tech media, high- and low-tech warfare methods, etc.

The term *netwar* refers to an emerging mode of conflict (and crime) at societal levels, short of traditional military warfare, in which the protagonists use network forms of organization and related doctrines, strategies, and technologies attuned to the information age. These protagonists are likely to consist of dispersed organizations, small groups, and individuals who communicate, coordinate, and conduct their campaigns in an internetted manner, often without precise central command . . . (N)etwar is about the Zapatistas more than the Fedelistas, Hamas more than the PLO, the American Christian Patriot movement more than the Ku Klux Klan, and the Asian Triads more than the Cosa Nostra.

—Arquilla and Ronfeldt[10]

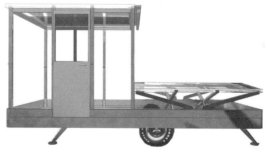

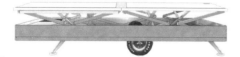

Deployed unit with high velocity

Deployed unit with medium velocity

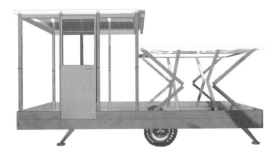

Their redundancy — that is, their ability to use multiple paths to produce the same result — makes them far more resilient than more rigid and linear power structures. The more complex and diverse the communication methods of these political groups, the more robust and sophisticated the system becomes.

Communication of any information, whether from DNA to RNA to protein or from one political faction to another, depends very much on the reliability of the transaction. Mediating between scales and materials builds in possibilities for static and interference to occur in these highly reactive systems. As a result, these networks often are able to produce unpredictable results because information fails to transmit reliably and/or is transferred in unusual ways.

In terms of genetics, this means that responsiveness and diversity are built into genetic interaction. Genes communicate and operate in non-uniform ways: certain players are more important or influential than others, and there are always a number of different paths for process execution.

It also means that negotiating different media has varying degrees of reliability. Communication of chemical information across cell membranes or between DNA and proteins involves a complex set of very sensitive players, processes, and interactions. Interference and misinterpretation are far from impossible; the process is riddled with *maybes*, *probablys*, *likelys* and *potentials*.

In terms of non-biological networks, they also are surprising and mutate in ways that are difficult to predict or prevent, be it the guerilla tactics of the Zapatistas or the actions of much of Al Queda. Their systems rely on the ingenuity and action of the distributed members of the group. Unlike genetic information networks, interference masks the internal operation — *i.e.* intent and identity — of members rather than producing new results.

Structured Change

Kevin Kelly writes about the developing interest in systems of *controlled complexity*:

> (D)aily revolution, I predict, will be headed off by daily evolution . . . science and commerce now seek to capture change — to instill it in a structured way — so that it works steadily, producing a constant tide of micro-revolutions instead of dramatic and disruptive macrorevolutions. How can we implant change into the artificial so that it is both ordered and autonomous?
>
> —Kevin Kelly[11]

Kelly thinks that the future of digital systems is in streamlining and guiding network mutation in such a way that it produces mutation constructively. Controlled complexity, in embryonic stages, has already been implemented in some 3D computer animation programs. Kelly reports that Industrial Light and Magic, makers of the Jurassic Park movie, can use the same dinosaurs — with the correct cosmetic changes — in the Flintstones movie.

"(I)nside Dino will beat the same digital heart of T. Rex and Velociraptor — different bodies but the same dinosaurness."[12] The computer program that controls both cartoon and lifelike dinosaur bodies, although with slightly different parameters — size and gravity, for example — describes similar dinosaur-like behavior. While explicit rules guide each network node, their interaction yields surprising but consistently animal behavior.

Networks are systems of potential; they constantly remake and reorganize themselves and are inseparable from their operation. Networked conditions exist within the *yes, and* condition described by Rajchman, mediating both the virtual and the actual.

Mobile Exchange Units

These highly mobile, intensely variable structures enable and nurture new connections at multiple distance and time scales. They will be deployed near the San Diego/Tijuana border, a territory rife with large migrant populations, frequent licit — and illicit — commerce and highly disparate economic situations. These activators infect lands and communities in this region, piggybacking on existing infrastructures and enabling access to broader exchange networks.

Martha Merzig holds a Bachelor of Architecture and a Bachelor of Science in Building Science from Rensselaer Polytechnic Institute, where she was awarded the Ricketts Prize in 2002. Her entry in the Van Alen Institute Queens Plaza Competition, designed with John Riker, earned an honorable mention.

She has worked with MateriaLab in Troy, NY on their finalist entry in the 2001 PS1 Young Architects Competition: Paradise Island, as well as with Leeser Architecture on their proposal for the Eyebeam Atelier Museum of New Technology. Currently, Martha works as an architecture intern at M1/DTW in Detroit.

David Riebe and Ted Krueger advised *Rules of Engagement*, her Bachelor of Architecture thesis project. Brian Lonsway and Jefferson Ellinger were reviewers.

Deployed units with low velocity

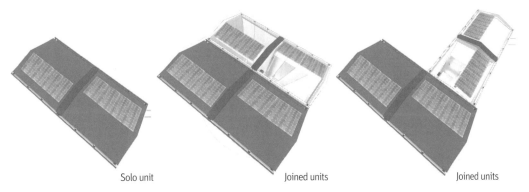

Solo unit   Joined units   Joined units

NOTES

1. Lewis, Michael. *Next: The Future Just Happened*. New York, NY: W.W. Norton & Co., 2001.
2. Gunther, Ingo. www.refugeerepublic.com
3. Ibid, Lewis.
4. Ibid, Lewis.
5. Tierney, John. "Here Come the Alpha Pups." *The New York Times Magazine*. August 5, 2001.
6. Osborne, Lawrence. "A Linguistic Big Bang." *The New York Times Magazine*. October 24, 1999.
7. Rajchman, John. "Artifice in an Ers@z World," *ANY 19/20*. Cynthia Davidson, ed., March 1997.
8. Rajchman, John. "The Virtual House: a Description," *ANY 19/20*. Cynthia Davidson, ed., March 1997.
9. Kelly, Kevin. *Out of Control: The Rise of Neo-Biological Civilization*. New York: Addison-Wesley, 1995.
10. Arquilla, John and David Ronfeldt, eds. *Networks and Netwars: The Future of Terror, Crime, and Militancy*. Santa Monica, CA: RAND Corporation, 2001.
11. Ibid, Kelly.
12. Ibid, Kelly.

ETHER: AN ARCHITECTURE OF SELF-NEGATION

the Architecture Urbanism Design
Collaborative (AUDC)

Los Angeles and the Theology of Ether

In *Empire*, Antonio Negri and Michael Hardt describe the new world order created by the global spread of capital. If national governments are withering away under the deterritorializing and liquefying forces of capitalism, Negri and Hardt claim that a new sovereignty is emerging, a transnational order they call Empire. This diffuse network supplants the old imperial model of center and periphery, replacing it with a placeless network of flows and hierarchies.

Empire is not ruled by one country, one people, or one place. Instead its force emanates from the global planetary network itself. Imperial sovereignty functions through three tiers that serve as checks and balances on each other while extending its power to all realms: monarchy, aristocracy, and democracy. These forms of sovereignty correspond to the Bomb; U.S. military superiority and nuclear supremacy — Money ; the economic wealth of the G7 — and Ether; the realm of the media, culture, and the global telecommunication networks. Although these tiers are placeless — any momentary fixities are quickly destabilized by the deterritorializing nature of Empire itself — Hardt and Negri suggest that *new Romes* appear to control them: Washington DC for the Bomb, New York for Money, and Los Angeles for Ether.

Over the last eighteen months, AUDC has investigated the historically most advanced form of imperial sovereignty, ether.

Like the now legendary medical substance, ether has an anesthetic quality. It separates the mind from the body, and reduces the dominance of physical sensation while maintaining the consciousness of the patient. Under the spell of its influence, the most intimate and cherished of all physical space, that of the body itself, can be assaulted at will. The use of ether to reduce pain in childbirth was originally banned by the Church, which argued that the suffering of Original Sin should not be relieved.

Los Angeles is the center of production for ether. Hollywood, as both a mythic place and a mode of production, is the telematic inhaler for the rest of the world, a sponge so soaked and saturated with ether that it can anesthetize the entire world.

Now that we have Los Angeles, we no longer need cities. Los Angeles has been designed as a giant stage set, ready for broadcast. It can become any city either known or imagined and can be exported to any location.

The Palace of the Empire of Ether

If the empire of ether were to have a palace, it would have to be the 39-story One Wilshire tower in downtown Los Angeles. Constructed at the apogee of modernism by Skidmore Owings and Merrill, One Wilshire unequivocally declares that form follows function. Perhaps the worst building SOM ever designed — excusable only as a product of the provincial San Francisco office — One Wilshire appears to follow only two guiding principles. First, in order to create a visual identity, One Wilshire was designed as a tower. Second, One Wilshire's window areas were maximized to provide light and views for the occupants. Throughout the design, expression of any form, including the expression of structure, was eliminated as superfluous. One Wilshire is the pure modernist building. Its neutral grid lacks symbolic content, making it a tower without qualities.

In his essay "The Fluid Metropolis," (*Domus* 496, March 1971) Andrea Branzi tracks the downfall of the skyscraper and the urban core. He observes that "the skyline becomes a diagram of the natural accumulation which has taken place of capital itself." Once capital takes over "the empty space in which [it] expanded during its growth period" and when "no reality exists any longer outside of the system," the skyscraper's representation of the accumulation of capital becomes obsolete. Branzi concludes that the horizontal factory and the supermarket — in which the circulation of information is made optimum and hierarchies disappear — would replace the tower as the foundational typologies for the fluid metropolis.

Branzi is, of course, correct. The increasingly horizontal corporation, organized along super-Taylorist and cybernetic principles of communicational efficiency, would construct low, spreading buildings for its offices in the suburbs. Consequently, in Los Angeles as in other cities, the congested vertical urban core had begun to empty. One Wilshire's once beneficial vertical signification of *office building* and *valuable real estate* began to get in the way of its own economic sustainability. By the mid-1980s, One Wilshire was obsolete. Fifteen years ago, however, a new opportunity presented itself and One Wilshire's height came to its advantage. With the deregulation of the telecommunications industry, MCI required a tall structure on which to install microwave antennas that would be in close proximity to Pacbell's Grand Street central switching station. One Wilshire was ideal for this task.

Other telecommunications companies soon joined MCI at One Wilshire, installing microwave antennas on the roof and renting space inside for their switching equipment. Over time the higher capacity of fiber optic lines allowed this technology to predominate over microwaves for long distance transmissions. By this point, however, the number of telecom companies with equipment in One Wilshire made it the main telecommunications hub for the city. Fiber optic lines crossing the continent and the ocean now routinely terminate at One Wilshire.

Over 120 telecom-related companies have installed equipment in the building. On One Wilshire's fourth floor, carriers freely run cables to transfer signals between each other. By avoiding costly intermediaries, carriers are save tremendous amounts of money and, in exchange, pay rent of $250 a square foot a month for this space. According to its managers, One Wilshire is the most expensive space to lease in all of North America.

None of these new functions of One Wilshire register on its façade. The space of global technological flows does not desire to become visual or apparent. Having no need of the physical and lacking an exterior to itself, ether has no need to appear.

Ugly and Ordinary

For the most part, One Wilshire is an ugly and ordinary building, akin to the now classic postmodernist retirement home, Guild House. In designing Guild House, Robert Venturi and Denise Scott Brown decided to avoid the monument and instead build a structure more appropriate to the banal demands of modern life. Cut-rate detailing and low-cost prefabricated elements made Guild House a stark reminder that modernism won its battle not because of ideology but because it was

cheaper to build than neo-classicism. Later projects by the firm that followed this methodology would be condemned as "ugly and ordinary" by Skidmore Owings and Merrill's lead designer Gordon Bunshaft. Venturi and Brown have adopted Bunshaft's term as a virtue, countering that ugly and ordinary items in culture represent the democratic segment of society, as they embody mass consciousness.

Choosing to strike preemptively against the ill-suited signage that clients inevitably put atop modernist buildings, Venturi and Scott Brown added their own sign to announce the structure's name: a second-rate panel that simply states *Guild House* above the entrance. At the top of the building the architects also mounted a non-functioning, gold anodized antenna to mark the building's common room and to signify that the elderly watch a lot of TV. Seen by both critics and occupants as a cynical joke at the expense of the inhabitants, this useless antenna was later removed.

The antenna's removal was not, however, a fatal blow. Venturi and Scott Brown observed that the ability to remove or replace signage at will gave flexibility to structures. Upon return from a research trip to Las Vegas, the architects would coin the term the *decorated shed* to refer to a modernist universal space coupled with a sign. In the decorated shed both function and meaning could be changed at will. Although Guild House is held by many to be a key building in the evolution of postmodernism, the ideas of the decorated shed and ugly and ordinary architecture proved too controversial for even the most avant-garde architects and Venturi and Scott Brown were virtually ostracized from the profession.

Like Guild House, One Wilshire is simply a neutral shell lacking any aesthetic gestures. There is no reason to think that Bunshaft wouldn't have called One Wilshire ugly and ordinary as well. It was constructed at almost the same time as Guild House and shares many of its features. It too is a decorated shed and has its own second-rate sign. Banal modernist lettering across its façade announces *One Wilshire* to the rest of the city.

Although the antennas at One Wilshire originally had a purpose, they are now also superfluous, empty symbols of a retired modern technology. As if in anticipation of the obsolescence of these antennas, One Wilshire goes a step further than the decorated shed: its signage is obsolete

from the start so it will never need to be removed. The building's real address is actually not One Wilshire, but 624 South Grand. An unbridgeable gap between signifier and signified, between form and function opens up at One Wilshire.

That this architecturally meritless structure is also the most valuable real estate in North America only confirms that the role of the building as a producer of effect or meaning is obsolete.

Immaterial Culture

Where Guild House was a home for the elderly, One Wilshire is the home in which we dwell telematically. Just as the elderly watched television in Guild House as a way of checking out of the weariness of life, we check into the global space of telecommunications in order to escape the dead world of objects. In both cases, however, the desire is to leave behind this world of material goods for something more pure, and to escape our responsibility to them by submitting to something greater.

The telecommunicational realm promises that the spirit can finally part from flesh and exist fully in a world of electronic images. These images are seductive because, circulating endlessly in an ethereal world, they cannot be possessed. We can fantasize about having such images to no end without ever feeling the disappointing responsibility of ownership.

Real objects are quickly known and classified. They give themselves up too easily. Like potential lovers, once they are purchased, objects become dead to our desires, lifeless pieces of junk.

Before late capitalism, objects had meaning because they were necessary but scarce. In our affluent society, however, objects are over-abundant, becoming merely components within a system of exchange without any clear use value to determine their price. The very basis of late capitalism presupposes the decoupling of currencies from the gold standard or any other guarantor of value. Today money proliferates wildly even as it means nothing.

There is no longer a clear logic to the system of capital. The dot.com boom, beanie babies, and today's inflated real estate values demonstrate this clearly. Value itself does not come out of any deeper truth but is constructed by temporary notions and mass delusions. This is a defensive measure for capital, so that massive run-ups in markets and unprecedented collapses can occur without any real consequence to the larger economy.

As the logic of our daily lives becomes increasingly removed from the direct consequences of our actions, objects are marketed and sold for their symbolic values alone. A teapot by Philippe Starck costs more because of its styling, even though it doesn't really work. But even the styling doesn't really matter, only Starck's name as a marker of value.

The increasing role of telecommunications and computers in everyday life does not do away with objects. Far from it, in immaterial culture physical objects proliferate endlessly even as they have become obsolete. Physical objects carry value only at moments of exchange: the moment they become so desirable that you want to purchase them and the moment that you can no longer tolerate their presence and want to get rid of them.

We still feel the need to own objects, even if the gratitude of ownership is fleeting. But physical objects will always repel us because they relentlessly fail to satisfy our desire to negate ourselves, to lose ourselves in their whispered promises. The on-again and off-again emotions we have about our objects confuse us, leaving us bewildered and lost. Our love for objects is routinely replaced by a deep hate. We sell them relentlessly on EBay but still they accumulate, contributing nothing to our lives. Every day more debt, more things, less joy.

We will never find a release from the need to own. Even if we can't sustain the gratitude of ownership, we purchase goods to validate our identity and diversity as individuals existing outside of this media web. But more than that, in submitting ourselves as willing slaves to our world of useless objects, we hope to become as disposable to them as they are to us today. We hope to be as ethereal and meaningless to them as they are to us. We hope that we will be allowed to leave this material world and dissipate in ether. And yet, as conflicted beings, we also hope that one day our objects will invest in us the same animistic beliefs with which we invest them. This is not our nightmare, it is the utopian dream in its achieved form, presence without purpose or responsibility, a slacker response of ambivalence and helplessness. The dream of immaterial culture is revenge on the world of objects.

The Becoming Unreal of the Real

The virtual is generally perceived as a drive against the spatial, or physical world. Nevertheless, the virtual world requires an infrastructure that exists in the physical and spatial world. Though ether is formless, it has to be created. Its production requires an enormous amount of physical hardware and consistent expertise.

Because of this, ether is primarily produced at nodes and locations where key players can meet and collect in front of, and behind cameras and computers. Massive telecommunicational urban hubs like One Wilshire and their radial networks make the virtual world possible, and firmly ground it into the concrete cityscape. Once this raw data of ether is created, it has to be stored and organized through stable control centers. These control centers, filled with row after row of servers generate an enormous amount of heat and require vast cooling systems with multiple back-up power units in order to function without interruption. Constant monitoring of these systems is vital as interruptions affect the entire system. Once the data has been collected, it has to be distributed outside of the building. Fiber optic cable is currently the most effective way of transmitting large quantities of data from out of the building into to the rest of the world. This cable is expensive to lay and requires a significant negotiation of both civic, private, and even international property as when fiber crosses national boundaries.

Telecommunication companies cannot afford all of these investments individually and have opted to pool their resources at a single location providing connectivity close to the transmission source. Through One Wilshire, virtually all of the global market leaders share a physical investment on the West Coast. Being *plugged in* is their literal need, not just an abstract notion.

Precisely because One Wilshire is tied to this physical location, it undermines the concept of an autonomous virtuality, revealing instead the simultaneous importance and abandonment of the physical world. In short, all of media and all of virtual life may be transmitted through non-physical technologies, but it is not possible to catalogue or store it without ties to storage and material culture. One Wilshire is an unimportant building without any physical presence or ability to signify its function as the palace of the empire of ether. Yet it is crucial. One Wilshire is the unreal exposing and making real of the unreal.

Individuals also long to become virtual and escape into ether. It is through this physical apparatus that, Hollywood stars, celebrities, and criminals obtain another body, a media life. Neither sacred or living, this media life is pure image, more consistent and dependable than physical life itself. It is the dream we all share: that we might become objects, or better yet, images. Media life can potentially be preserved for eternity, cleansed of unscripted character flaws and accidents — a guaranteed legacy that defies aging and death by already appearing dead on arrival. The idols of millions via magazines, film, and television are precisely these disembodied, lifeless forms without content or meaning.

But the terrifying truth is that, although the media image itself may be eternal, its host is prone to destruction and degradation. Data itself is not free of physicality. When it is reduplicated or backed up to file and stored via a remote host it suffers the same limitations as the physical world. It can be erased, lost, and compromised. The constant frustration of CDs, DVDs, and hard drives is that they don't last forever, and all data is lost at once. Up to 20% of the information carefully collected on Jet Propulsion Laboratory computers during NASA's 1976 Viking mission to Mars has been lost. The average Web page lasts only a hundred days, the typical life span of a flea on a dog. Even if data isn't lost, the ability to read it soon disappears. Photos of the Amazon Basin taken by satellites in the 1970s are critical to understanding long-term trends in deforestation but are trapped forever on indecipherable magnetic tapes.

Ether is the Medium of Self-Negation

That the dot.com and telecom busts occurred in the first year of the new millennium is no accident. Those who participated and invested in these busts acted irrationally, but not without reason. Like the followers of the Heaven's Gate cult and those who hoped that the year 2000, or better yet, a Kubrickesque 2001 would mark the end of all things, they were just desperate to believe that the end was near. The process of investing in Pets.com was a matter of giving oneself up. Borrowing on margin to invest not only the entirety of one's pension in Akamai or Worldcom but to generate a life-crushing debt as a form of voluntary slavery.

The pundits were mistaken: it was not that we all hoped to get out of the boom before it failed, it was that we wanted to be part of its failure and to feel its destruction. The greatest disappointment of the dot.com crash of 2000 was its failure to bring about the promise of the dot.com era: the end of all things. Today, Rem Koolhaas and other members of the post-avant-garde maintain that architecture should do nothing more than embody the flows of capital.

Instead of enslaving itself to capital, as it does now, and instead of fulfilling the master-slave dialectic to become capital's master, as it always wished to be under modernism, architecture now decides to end the game and achieve oneness with capital. If achieving a state of oneness with capital is architecture's fantasy, what better place for this to happen than at One Wilshire? If architecture is to become capital, it will do so by becoming ether. This is only possible when architecture loses all sense of intrinsic value and enters into a pure system of exchange.

Technology allows architecture to dissociate itself from any specific interior condition and to become one with ether. Through symbol libraries and the magic of the .dxf import command, it has become possible for architectural plans to reproduce at will. The toilet rooms from Frank

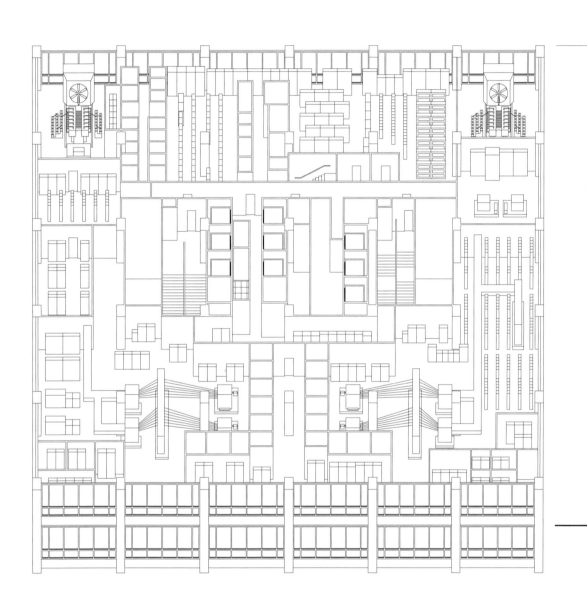

Gehry's signature building, the Guggenheim Museum at Bilbao, can be copied onto a CD-ROM by an intern to endlessly re-appear in schools of architecture worldwide, their first role in life irrelevant and forgotten. In this light, the prevalence of the computation-intensive blob in the academy is revealed as the product of fear, a desperate attempt to reintroduce the hand and slow down architectural production just at the moment that as it threatens to proliferate wildly, allowing architecture to become pure ether.

One Wilshire has no such fear. Created before the dawn of computer-aided design, it transcends architecture as pure diagram and pure Idea. Endlessly replicable, there is no limit to its potent reach. It is the architectural realization of Hegel's Spirit itself. One Wilshire is a masterpiece of terror. It is an architecture of pure self-negation, simultaneously real and virtual, visible and unseen. One Wilshire is the palace for the empire of ether.

AUDC
Begun as a research unit within the Southern California Institute of Architecture (SCI-ARC), Architecture Urbanism Design Collaborative is a nonprofit organization dedicated to using the tools of architecture to research the role of the individual and the community in the contemporary urban environment.

Founding Members
Robert Sumrell teaches in the architecture program at Woodbury University. Robert's research focuses on how architecture can help articulate the individual in mass-produced society. He is a scholar of the 1960s Italian anti-design movement as well as 1980s furniture by Memphis and is also interested in sustainable design, sprawl, and theology.

Kazys Varnelis has a doctorate in the History of Architecture and Urbanism from Cornell University and teaches in the Southern California Institute of Architecture's history-theory faculty. His research spans the history of cities, the influence of telecommunications on urbanity, nature and ecology, and late modern architecture.

LIVE FROM EVERYWHERE TO EVERYWHERE ALL THE TIME FOREVER

CNN'S WORLD INFORMATION REGIME

Daniela Fabricius

In an age of decentralization and supposed liberation of information through the Internet there are still vast infrastructures largely controlled by very few players. CNN, taken as a case study, reveals a set of new infrastructures and relationships, which are in constant emergence. The brand represents a crucial node in the panoply of communications that have covered the globe in the last 20 years. While nobody could convincingly argue that this is not much more than yet another stage in the continuing development of the global activities of information exchange, it is one that comes close to fulfilling a diverse number of modernist paradigms that have shadowed us from the early 20th century onward. These visions and ideologies, with authors as diverse as Marshall McLuhan, Marconi, the Russian Constructivists, Arthur C. Clarke, and Buckminster Fuller, proposed a system of worldwide communication as a way to create a coordination of markets, politics, cultures, revolutions, and natural resources.

CNN is posited on a diverse set of axes: the U.S. military, satellite infrastructures, financial networks, global film and print industries, telecommunications, advertising, the United Nations, and national governments. To map the levels of connectivity in which CNN operates is to reveal both the breadth and homogeneity of global communications.

While the World Wide Web has been responsible for moving and storing an impressive mass of data, much of it residual, CNN has been in the business of creating, marketing, and distributing information, thought by many to be the most important commodity today. The penetration of this information network is unprecedented, as is the speed at which information can be retrieved and disseminated. While much attention has been given to the internet, television and radio still have a far greater audience and influence on political and economic events. The most recent stages in deregulation and liberalization of global media have placed this influence in the hands of very few.

New Territories

Access to satellite bandwidth was largely responsible for CNN's dramatic growth. Since their inception, the use of satellites for navigation, cellular phones, weather and geological information, news broadcasting, and military intelligence, has been posing new challenges to the notions of territorial borders and spaces. The first satellites date from the era of the space race, when Russia inched ahead with the launching of Sputnik in 1957. This was soon followed by the first communications satellite, launched in 1961, and the first use of satellites for broadcasting television during the 1964 coverage of the Tokyo Olympics. INTELSAT, a treaty organization among nations, was an IGO (intergovernmental organization) created in 1964 to regulate the use of and fair access to satellites. With UNESCO, it sought to secure the use of satellites for educational projects in developing nations. The restrictions posed by these regulations led the U.S. and Great Britain, who had historically dominated global communications industries, to withdraw from UNESCO in 1985.

Today, access to satellite television is completely determined by the logic of entertainment. India, it is estimated, has increased its number of satellite TV subscribers from 3,000 to 1 million in just the past 3 years. In certain regions, the Arab world in particular, satellite television has bypassed two previous barriers to communication: illiteracy and government censorship. Governments cannot physically stop the satellite signals from being beamed into their regions, and legislation controlling international satellite communication has all but been eradicated. Governments as diverse as Canada, Iraq, and Vietnam, have attempted to ban the sale and ownership of satellite receivers, but they are largely unsuccessful in the face of a thriving black market and almost total public resistance. Only 50 years ago the Soviet Union jammed radio waves from the United States and Europe with no less than 3000 separate radio transmissions dedicated to that purpose. Only five years ago the use of satellites was regulated by an international consortium (INSTELSAT), while today transmission space is open to the highest bidder.

From Atlanta to the World

Unlike the BBC, which had its origins in radio, CNN was an entirely new concept from the beginning. The idea of a superstation, a 24-hour news network, independent from the existing major networks in the U.S., and available only to private subscribers, was met with ridicule when it was first suggested by Ted Turner in 1980. CNN came out of a period in American broadcasting when the coverage of the Vietnam War had given the American press a sense of autonomy in the reporting of conflicts. The 1970s were also a time when shifting economic interdependence led to the development of simultaneous smaller conflicts, fought by guerillas and terrorists, as opposed to the formality of a clearly defined theater of war. Ted Turner, with the support of the UN and Jimmy Carter, envisioned CNN as part of the global communications utopia, through which he could "bring world peace and get rich in the process."[1] *World Report* was originally slated to be broadcast from the UN headquarters in New York. UNTV is still one of the biggest contributors to *World Report*, and Ted Turner is a

big contributor to the UN: he recently donated a record $1 billion.

Currently, CNN has the capability to report from and broadcast to every part of the globe. CNN's international sphere began modestly with offices in London and Rome. But it was the launch of *World Report* in 1987 that brought it into a new conceptual paradigm. *World Report* was based on a simple premise: anybody, any station, anywhere in the world, could send in a tape 2.5 minutes in length, reporting on local conditions, and it would be broadcast uncensored. The idea that local conditions halfway across the world would be broadcast to an American audience was a radically new experiment in global space. Enormous technological differences had to be overcome in order for countries with limited technologies and infrastructures to get a tape sent to Atlanta, often through an informal network of bribes, favors, and good luck.

What these relationships achieved, more importantly, was the establishment of an extra-governmental network of international exchange and information dissemination which would give CNN unprecedented access and coverage to previously inaccessible areas in the world. While technology for immediate communication did not yet exist, *World Report* was able to forge relationships with other networks and news organizations which would become the backbone of CNN's global territory. This territory now includes 39 international bureaus and 900 international affiliates, sharing content, coverage, and equipment with CNN via 38 satellites. CNN was granted access to places like Cuba — where it staged the first live U.S. telecast since 1958 — and Russia, which during the sensitive year of 1985 allowed the American network to set up a bureau in Moscow. Incidentally, this was around the time that Russian jamming of world radio signals ceased, and only a few years before the communist empires would collapse in a domino effect fueled by coverage provided by CNN. The gravity of this process is illustrated in the words spoken by Gorbachev in 1991 during the signing of his own resignation. During the ceremony, broadcast exclusively by CNN, Gorbechev's pen had run out of ink. CNN president Tom Johnson lent him his own Mont Blanc, and Gorbechev jokingly said to him "You've built your empire better than I built mine."[2]

Narrowcasting

By 1993 CNN's global viewership had matched its U.S. audience. Today, according to CNN, its constellation of channels are viewed by 1 billion people worldwide in more than 200 countries and territories in 8 different languages through household subscribers, hotel rooms, embassies,

airports, and hospitals. Furthermore, its Web sites receive 1 billion hits per month. Thus, in the space of little more than 10 years, CNN has evolved from a network bringing international news to the United States, to a U.S. based network bringing news to the world.

As decentralized as its infrastructures may appear, all news first channels through CNN headquarters in Atlanta, before it is *re*transmitted out into the world. CNN is headquartered in a building that was once a shopping mall, situated along a freeway and next to a stadium, where the control rooms house CNN's staff. They work long delirious hours, barely sleeping during times of war, unable to stop monitoring the news.

It is not long, however, when a critical point is reached when trying to provide a global, 24-hour station to differing time zones, cultural interests and local conditions — it is always primetime somewhere. CNN's content and format has transformed from broadcasting to narrowcasting: The monolithic news service has fragmented into specialty interests — CNNfinancial, CNNsports, etc.), with 14 different networks featuring distinct continental, even national programming (CNNTurk), niche advertising and localized content. One can only imagine further fragmentation into customized news consumption as it is already marketed on the Internet, or services like CNN Mobile which delivers custom news to cell phones and PDAs. While earlier satellite technology was more costly, making wide-range homogenized programming cost-effective, technology now is able to deliver on demand content. Geostationary satellite coverage can range from a very broad hemisphere signal (at 35,000 feet above the earth), to a focused spot beam, which allows the user to send a signal to a specific area, as small as a city. This has allowed CNN to further specify niche areas for advertising revenues, and to control who sees which programs.

Everyone is a Potential Reporter

The tendency towards optimization is taking place in the retrieval of news as well. While in the first Gulf War, reporters were confined to using flyaways weighing 3000 pounds and costing around $250,000; reporters now use a small satellite videophone and a $500 DVD camera, which can be solar-powered, allowing for unprecedented mobility. The media is able to provide streaming content live from anywhere in the world, with picture and sound — the first Gulf War did not have real-time video — even from a moving vehicle. The journalist is as light and mobile as the soldiers with whom he or she is embedded. Journalists are not dependent on local infrastructures — which may have been destroyed — and their presence is more transparent than ever, as many recording devices are so small and unfamiliar that they can be easily concealed. The use of these light and inexpensive technologies means not only wider and faster coverage — albeit with a lower bandwidth), but it also means that broadcasting technologies themselves will soon be available to a wider audience. The amateur videos of 9/11 and, most famously, the Rodney King videotape have proved that everyone is a potential reporter. This will be especially true when DVD and video tapes no longer have to be sent, but rather can be posted online or streamed directly, and devices as small as cellphones equipped with cameras can be used to digitally send images around the world. Around the world, in this case, means back to Atlanta. While these devices will begin to undermine the technological dominance of Big News (*i.e.* CNN, the BBC, etc.), perhaps allowing for other news sources, it could also render the established networks ever more powerful, pushing the original concept of a *World Report* to a new level in which information is constantly being gathered and rebroadcast to the world from more and more sources, although always through the same channels.

While CNN's internal infrastructures are vast, it is like many global news sources dominated by a handful of players. CNN is owned by Turner Broadcasting, which (since 1996), is owned by Time Warner, which, with an annual revenue of $27Billion, is the largest media conglomerate in the world. Its board of directors includes, among others, the heads — and former heads — of AOL, Colgate-Palmolive, Phillip Morris, Fannie Mae, Hilton Hotels, AT&T, FedEx, Sun Microsystems, a former U.S. Trade ambassador, and Vincent Enterprises. Vincent Enterprises provides communications technology for military unmanned reconnaissance planes and cruise missiles. Conspiracy theorists exhaust themselves trying to trace all of these connections within corporate hierarchies, while the public is less and less surprised by these inbred relationships between broadcast media and industry.

CNN also operates within yet another global infrastructure — that of the news agency and image industry. CNN, like BBC, and many other news sources, does not rely only on its own reporters, but on news services such as the Associated Press, Agence Française de Presse and Reuters. These news agencies, whose influence should not be overlooked, collectively provide in excess of 90% of international news content to over 2 billion people, managing vast photo, video, word, and financial information banks whose contents are sold to newspapers, Web sites, and television networks around the world. These companies, which have been battling anti-trust suits for almost a century, are, like the major news networks, also based in the U.S. and UK. The one exception is Agence Française de Presse. So, while CNN began by establishing an autonomous and diverse global infrastructure, it is now part of a market which is becoming increasingly media rich and information-poor.

CNN has also had to forge a close and complicated relationship with the U.S. military through its coverage of wars. The military's official stance toward the media was irrevocably shaped by the Vietnam War, when the idea was perpetuated that full access to the experience of war, if left uncensored, would bring about a loss of support from the American people. The Gulf War, which made CNN famous, had the most relentless, yet limited coverage of war in televised history. CNN broadcast an unprecedented 900 uninterrupted hours of coverage, much of it live. While CNN had gained the trust of the Iraqis, it was also working closely with the military in the states, with several military analysts on call full-time and PSYOPS (psychological operations) personnel on staff. It was during this conflict that the operations and techniques of the media mirrored that of the military in new ways. It was the Gulf War that gave us the famous military-provided images of cameras mounted onto smart bombs which exploded without showing the aftermath, night-vision footage, computer simulations and reenactments, satellite signal jamming and censorship, and strategic disinformation provided by the military. We never saw bodies. The U.S. military provided CNN with the footage of the precision bombs which later turned out to comprise only 8% of the missiles used, and it deliberately misled reporters in an attempt to fool enemy leaders who were ostensibly watching CNN for their information.

This trend toward military control of information has escalated during the current Iraq war. In order to advertise and familiarize the war, the military decided to allow so-called *embedded journalists* to accompany military divisions. The journalists were given full 24-hour access to the military and its movements, in exchange for almost full power by the military to censor the information. The result was a cinematic, reality-television version of war geared toward home and enemy viewers alike. CNN has been placed in the role of supplying a crucial component of the military's greater information strategy.

C5I

According to many military analysts, we are currently in 4th generation of asymmetrical warfare, in which technology superiority is no longer what makes you a winner — an example would be the recent attack on a Baghdad hotel by a missile launched from a donkey cart — nor does there necessarily need to be a winner. What was once called C3 — *command, control, communications* — is now C4I — add *computers* and *information*

Daniela Fabricius received a Master in Architecture from Columbia University in 2003. She has worked on numerous books and exhibitions, including *Mutations*, which she co-authored with Sanford Kwinter. In 2001, she worked at the office of Martin/Baxi Architects where she contributed to a multidisciplinary project called "Timeline: A Retroactive Masterplan for Silicon Valley, 1950-2050." She currently has her own research and design practice, and is the editor of an upcoming book and exhibition on Brazil's informal urban settlements.

NOTES

1. Flournoy, Don F. and Robert K. Stewart. *CNN: Making New in the World Market*, University of Luton Press, 1997.
2. Ibid, Flournoy and Stewart.
3. Taylor, Philip M. *Global Communications, International Affairs and the Media Since 1945*, Routledge, 1997.
4. Ibid, Taylor.
5. El-Nawawy, Mohammed and Adel Iskandar, *Al Jazeera*, Cambridge: Westview Press, 2003.

All images are courtesy of NASA, except CNN logo, courtesy of CNN.

— or, as some have jokingly put it, C5I, the final *C* standing for CNN. As George H.W. Bush once said, "I get more information from CNN than I do from the CIA."[4] What the military has lost is control over information and opinion, and CNN clearly holds the monopoly. With its vast informal networks, communications infrastructure, corporate backing, brand recognition, and diversified markets, CNN has created a far more effective form of penetration. Research conducted by CNN has shown that its audience is comprised largely of influential people — CEOs, investors, politicians, diplomats — and CNN is their primary information source on global matters. CNN moves at a speed that is "faster than diplomacy,"[3] creating enormous pressure on politicians to make crucial decisions with a speed that was unthinkable even 30 years ago. Policy decisions on Bosnia and Somalia, and the collapse of the Soviet Empires were believed to have been largely influenced by what was or was not shown on CNN.

Live from the Country of Goats

While it is not a direct product of the U.S. government, as the Voice of America radio stations were after WWII, CNN now is considered by many to represent exclusively American political interests and values. After CNN became the only international station with continuous coverage of the Gulf War, a group in the Middle East responded, forming the Al Jazeera news station in 1996. Located in Qatar, (derided as a "country of goats"[5]), Al Jazeera posed a serious and important challenge to the dominance of CNN. With almost all of its budget going toward equipment, Al Jazeera has become the most-watched network in the Middle East, with women selling their jewelry to buy satellite dishes and to gain access to it. It has agitated Western and conservative Islamic regimes alike, who find the service either too radical or too modern. Yet United States intelligence has come to rely on the news station for leads on terrorists and issues in the Middle East. Many world leaders use it to communicate with the Arab world both in the region and in diaspora. Al Jazeera is one example of what may be a growing trend in global news. As the technology for reporting and distributing news becomes less expensive and smaller in size, and the prices for satellite time fall, the possibilities for smaller, local networks to broadcast internationally will increase. This would certainly create a new stage in global networks, one which will no doubt create more noise and more data, as well as new information regimes.

LEARNING FROM WALL STREET

DYNAMIC STRATEGIES OF
PRODUCTION AND PRACTICE

Beth Blostein

Dynamic Realities

In *The City in History*, Lewis Mumford noted in the early 1960s the entropic spread of cities due to changing economic, cultural, and social forces, a phenomenon indescribable at that time by any method of mapping or representation.[1] Following shortly behind were the first digital images of the Earth, taken in 1972 by NASA satellites. These raster images were some of the first publicly disseminated artifacts of the Digital Age. Beyond the novelty of digital imaging technology, the truth assigned to photography — digital or analog — fostered the mass dissemination of these images as one of the earliest incidences of global data consumption. The full impact of the digital nature of these images was not then realized; these images of the Earth allowed scientists, by studying changes in the digital array, to uncover weather patterns and transformations in the planet's surface. This construct yielded more information than traditional methods of imaging ever could, allowing for recognition of multiple realities. Curiously, technologies can both reveal inherently dynamic conditions and provide impetus for them. Consider these later examples:

> Through satellite imaging, the U.S. Department Office of International Information monitors patterns of deforestation in the countries of Columbia, Bolivia, and Peru. Certain patterns indicate the replacement of indigenous vegetation with illicit drug crops such as coca and opium poppy.[2]

> The July 19, 2001 edition of the Denver Post reported on the acquittal of Patrick Murphy, who was accused of misdemeanor harassment for using satellite mapping to track the patterns of dog excrement at a nearby playground and then confronting negligent owners.[3]

Following closely behind the revelation of coexistent worldviews enabled by imaging technologies was the public emergence of information and communications technologies of the early 1980s. Minitel, the French version of the Internet, was created by the French national government in an effort to promote sanctioned social and political interactions via networked information. The system was originally a glorified phone book, the hardware distributed at a very low cost or for free. However, as is the case with many technologies — its cultural context produced unexpected user dynamics, spawning spontaneous and highly flexible organizational patterns. The system fostered extended markets for pornographic and political propaganda, drawing international attention in 1985 after the entire system crashed due to high volumes of lewd activity.

Today our world is connected though a complex web of transnational networks. The internet, the primary generator of these networks, is the medium that allows us to communicate and interact regardless of physical proximity. The information driving these complex relationships is often unstructured, hard to find, and dynamic. To sift through and map relationships between nodes and networks, mathematical models are used that employ fuzzy logic — embedding factors of uncertainty, vagueness, and approximation.[4]

Available — and accessible — electronic information ranges from intelligence to supply chain reconnaissance to reputation data to consumer indices. The diversity and breadth of information available online is prized in the business sector, where successful organizations use it to achieve competitive advantage. Information capitalists literally deal in information — demographic data becomes consumer history, becomes credit ratings, becomes targeted advertisements — all awaiting sampling and interpretation. These digital commodities, produced and exchanged according to market demand, enable a hyper-extension of capitalism.[5]

While currently applied primarily in money and advantage-seeking ventures, mutable, consumer-driven operational strategies will ultimately characterize many types of organizations, including cultural and domestic ones. Trends in technology consumption reflect this fact. Novell estimates there are 200 billion microchips in use everyday with 145 microprocessor-controlled devices in every home. That amounts to thirty-five chips for each person on the planet. Computing is being freed from the obvious traditional devices and is being embedded in handheld, appliances, walls, clothes, and other domestic components. These devices mediate and modify every-day existence. The dynamics implied by the inclusion of these technologies as part of the quotidian suggests new inhabitational demands for architecture. However, architecture remains fixed in its attitude toward program and conventional construction methods, making it resistant to modification.

A Problematic State for Architecture

Mies van der Rohe thought that "true architecture is always objective and is the expression of the inner structure of our time, from which it stems."[6] At the beginning of the century, Le Corbusier's Maison Dom-ino House addressed the needs of an emerging European middle class by wedding the nascent modern aesthetic of abstraction to the developing technology of reinforced concrete. In the middle of the century, Frank Lloyd Wright's Usonian Houses adapted Jeffersonian ideals to an American suburban context through an inventive use of newly available, inexpensive dimensioned lumber. At the close of the century, the flowering cultural force of late capitalism is embodied by Frank Gehry's Bilbao Museum. From Corbusier to Wright to Gehry, both architectural theory and practice have been immersed in emerging social, aesthetic, functional, and technical concerns.

Current architectural practice, however, has a naïve relationship to contemporary hyper-capitalist culture. Architecture, the *mother of the arts*, has its historical basis in patron/beneficiary relationships, inherently insulating it from full involvement in current cultural dynamics. This separation, the antithesis of the engagement demonstrated by Corbusier, Wright, and Gehry, is a uniquely contemporary, yet disadvantageous position. The dynamic capacity required by financial ventures to continuously recalibrate efforts in response to changing communication, consumption or organizational patterns, has no counterpart in architectural practice. In fact, over time the architectural process has been denatured through segregation by the construction trade; the role of the architect has been relegated to one of producer of image. The architect's primary means of representation, the drawing, is an idealized abstraction. The construction process only approximates, using the means and methods defined by the trades, to embody the established ideals represented by the drawings.

There is also a lack of revolution in architectural products because there is a persistent image of stasis and stability associated with architectural work. But consider that while we once built for 50- to 100-year building life spans, today 25-year life spans are not uncommon. Recent trends in building demolition and booms in re-construction of professional sports venues, malls, and airports reveal civic and corporate attitudes about built work. Sports arenas are now financed in more fluid ways: luxury box sales and corporate naming rights demand continual upgrading of facilities. Malls promote fluctuating models of consumerism that necessitate new experiences. Airports constantly require new technologies that continually up the ante on the safety and efficiency to be accommodated by architecture. Each year, 44,000 relatively new commercial buildings are demolished, while 170,000 new ones are constructed.[7]

In the residential sector, a full 10% of single-family home owners relocated in the last year; nearly half reported the move was due to a variety of persistent or emergent inadequacies that their current home could not accommodate.[8] 92% of the 136 million tons of waste produced by the construction industry is from demolition.[9] Clearly, there are dangerous inadequacies in current architectural strategies — both culturally and physically. Mutable architectures that fluidly and seamlessly accept modification in response to changing conditions are much needed.

It has been suggested since the early 1990s, that computer-aided design systems and digital communications technologies would revolutionize the practice of architecture and provide a solution to this quandary. Highly accurate documents could be produced, modified, transmitted and cataloged quickly and efficiently, thus dematerializing geographic barriers. These predictions have been realized, though lacking true innovation. Until now the discourse has been concerned more with the computer's ability to represent a construction's singular truth: its dimensions, its materials, its lighting configurations, its view from eye level. But, as we have seen, actual living conditions exist somewhere between order and chaos. As such, there are limits to architecture's ability to frame these contexts at a human scale.

For the practice of architecture, the problem does not stem from an inability to produce or exchange information, but from the limited value and potential it attributes to that information. The discipline has not yet fully recognized the opportunities available to Information Capitalists whose ability to exploit digital information embeds a system of innovation and evolution in their products and practices.

The coincidence of the two problems — diminishment of the role of the architect and the need for a contemporary architecture — is ironic. However, the strategic application of technologies can redefine the architect's static methods of representation as mutable, market-driven commodities — commodities that critically respond to the needs and desires of contemporary culture.

Dynamic Practices

Technologies can be used to dynamically and continuously recalibrate our practices and products. In the early 1900s, led by artists including Peter Behrens, the discipline of industrial design capitalized on emerging technologies. It ensured its own future by inventing a consumer market for itself, aestheticizing the introduction of electricity into the home in the form of domestic appliances. Industrial design was strategically remade, inextricably tying it to all aspects of product: its form, function, engineering, materiality, safety assurance, and ultimately its continual innovation.

Architecture needs a similar reinvention. First, the practice itself needs to be addressed. In the last decade, digital technologies have been increasingly instrumental, now streamlining the processes of design and construction documentation. More radically, computer numerically controlled (CNC) production allows for the direct translation of computer modeling data to tool paths for fabrication; the tools take on a number of forms, from mills to glorified glue guns. The traditional rift between designer and producer is eliminated, time-to-market is reduced, and consumers are provided with multiple options within quality controls normally associated with one-off custom design. So, sketch = digital information = shop drawings = product.

Frank Gehry has led the way in the utilization of these techniques of production. But with his proposal for a 550,000 square foot Guggenheim Museum in lower Manhattan estimated at $900 million and now side-lined, the techniques are certainly not part of the quotidian.[10]

At almost the opposite end of the design spectrum from Gehry, the somewhat pragmatic task of facilities management exists: a less-than-glamorous, yet highly dynamic, model of operation enabled by computer technologies. A digital database becomes a comprehensive repository of information on an organization's people, places, processes, and physical assets. Access to this integrated information enables organizations to make strategic decisions that optimize return on investment, lower asset life cycle costs, and increase overall productivity and profitability. Light bulb outages can be mapped and repurchased through a system of dynamic links and databases. Energy consumption can be tracked. Moves of individuals or entire departments can be planned. A mega-conglomeration can be right-sized. This task, once the happenstance purview of the janitorial or an unlucky administrative staff, has established itself as a discipline complete with its own body of knowledge. This discipline changes the way buildings are inhabited by becoming a necessary partner for effective occupation, providing a continuous flow of value-added, albeit largely intangible, products.

In all sectors of society there are trends to do more with less, from corporate right-sizing to paper-use quotas to hybrid cars to calorie cutting. Recognizing the ability that digital information has

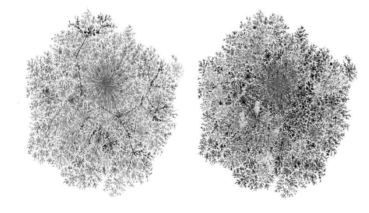
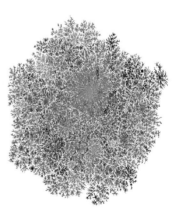

© Lumeta, Corp.

to embody numerous forms almost instantaneously, from drawings to operating instructions, opens the potential invention of new architectural products. But in order to utilize these new products, we must begin by redefining the architect/client relationship that has traditionally placed the architect in a provisional role of image-producer.

In actuality, architecture's efficacy is greatly hindered by often narrowly-defined boundaries established by this relationship. A conceptual divide exists between value assigned by the architect, versus that of the client, to the instruments of design — traditionally drawings and models. Often the product, or construction, is seen as the only thing that has quantifiable value. The instruments of its production are merely residual, items offered as collateral, as a temporary stand-in for the product. According to the AIA, only 4-6% of a project's cost goes into design and engineering services. Of that fee, less than half goes toward the schematic design and design development phases combined. The majority of clients simply don't want to pay for the intangibles — the conceptualizing, the thinking, the critiquing, the things that cannot be consumed. This divide is fostered by the power various trades wield by supplying a specific and tangible product. The plumbing contractor provides systems for waste removal, the electrical contractor provides systems for power.

In a dynamic architectural practice, the drawings become a mutable database that simultaneously records a work's history, controls its techniques of construction, while also inherently and seamlessly accommodating an undetermined future by providing a method of meeting inconstant needs. The traditional architectural product loses its terminal status and becomes a node within an overall and evolving, self-perpetuating service.

Just as the practice needs to do more, the need to ask buildings to do more goes hand-in-hand. In the United States, as much as one-third of the built environment will be torn down between now and 2025. But at the same time, at least one-half of the new construction needed to respond to population growth has yet to be constructed.[11]

We can find some inspiration for change in the dynamic potential suggested by D'Arcy Thompson's rubber sheet geometries. Thompson considered how mathematics could be applied to figures of one organism to transform it into another: within one figure lies the potential to become something else.[12] Thompson suggests that within the human lies the potential to become a baboon. This same analogy can be used to envision an architecture that responds to contemporary conditions. At some levels we must then reject the notion that a work of architecture must be programmatically, functionally, and contextually static.

This need for mutable, flexible, non-terminal practices perhaps goes hand-in-hand with the emergence of architectures that forgo form alone as a mode of investigation, favoring instead studies of unprogrammed yet highly functional spaces, such as that of the massive Yokohama International Port Terminal by Foreign Office Architects. But a great challenge facing contemporary architects is the question of how to re-invent the profession in such a way that it can influence the ordinary, everyday, commonplace buildings. Architects have failed to influence the construction sector in any significant way, as the demand for building consumes any and all architectural innovation.

To meet this burgeoning demand, most innovation takes place in the building system products industry. This industry relies on the mass production of building components, such as lighting systems, curtain walls, exterior insulation and finish systems, which come fully equipped with an established body of knowledge embedded in the systems themselves. These systems come with UL ratings, fire ratings, and other performance standards, as well as acceptable applications and details. Success in this industry goes hand-in-hand with issues ingrained during the industrial revolution of standardization, predictable performance, and legal issues of responsibility, so emphasized in a world of mega lawsuits. Unfortunately, unlike the models of Le Corbusier and Walter Gropius, the practice of architecture has been a passive participant in this multi-disciplinary global dynamic of production and distribution.

Selected at random, the September 2002 issue of *Architectural Record* has 384 pages — almost 33% is advertising. With hundreds of billions of dollars expended on it annually, advertising becomes a means of economic survival in all sectors.[13] Building systems become products that architects and designers consume. Because material and formal precedents and standards have been largely determined by these manufacturers, innovation occurs primarily in the ways these systems are arranged.

More promising, First Penthouse, a Swedish company founded by two civil engineers, produces ready-made apartments for London rooftops. Using three dimensional digital surveys and high-end manufacturing technologies, the existing conditions are mapped for which the company creates a customized penthouse. No two are the same. Furthermore, the project, installed in one day, is located on prime real estate. Enabled by digital technologies, built forms are strategically made for new territories.

What should inevitably follow from discussions such as this is a new way of manifesting a work of architecture. Architecture

needs to become a physically and conceptually flexible frame that receives the ineludible changes and fluctuations in modes of operation, in the form of upgrades, exchanges, and expansions within the confines of its walls, and in the form of skins and apertures, as a participant in an urban context. For architecture, the digital information that is already part and parcel of typical practice is no longer simply a means to an end, i.e. the production of a set of drawings. Clearly digital technologies and computer numerically controlled fabrication techniques have enabled the production of Frank Gehry's unique forms and First Penthouse's apartment structures. But with dynamic architectural practices and products, unlike Frank Gehry's forms, architecture is not resistant to reformulation or redefinition by a static steel under-belly.

We can consider the problem of housing as a specific example, as residential construction plays a vital role in the economy of the United States. It is estimated that this year a tremendous portion of the $872.2 billion value of new construction will be residential construction.[14]

By 2020, an additional 25 million households will be formed in the United States. Trends suggest that one's lifestyle will evolve multiple times during a lifetime; the face of those households will be non-traditional and variable. Nearly 12 million will be immigrant households where extended family comes and goes. Others will be unmarried couples, both hetero- and homosexual, and singles who marry later in life. An individual now changes jobs an average of six times throughout adulthood. These protean households are expected to make up as much as 70 percent of the population even by 2010.[15] What will be needed is domestic space that expands, contracts, and mutates in response to economic and lifestyle conditions. A dynamic architecture has systems — communications, plumbing, and building envelopes — that remain fixed yet ubiquitous. At the same time it has programs that can be expanded, upgraded, downgraded, or obliterated - bedrooms, bathrooms, mother-in-law suites. These programs become fluid extensions, or new architectural products, of the way dynamic architecture is practiced.

Accepting the Challenge of Wall Street

Virilio defines *stereo-reality* as, "a condition that can be obtained when the simultaneous presence of two dimensions—the real one and the virtual one — generates a completely new spatial and temporal *deepness* effect."[16] Digital global structures of information and communication have — and will continue to be — assimilated into our environments. The practice of architecture has the opportunity at this point to participate in the remaking of itself, capitalizing on the potential to build new markets by reordering static models of representation and fabrication. Demonstrated through the exploits of Information Capitalists, digital information — the new representational medium — is dynamic, can assume multiple forms and perform multiple tasks.

With growing trends to do more with less in conjunction with continually fluctuating needs, architects will have to find innovative ways to meet demands. Suddenly, the practice of architecture becomes dynamic and deals not with architecture as an end product, but as a continual service with multiple consequences, both material and immaterial. This goes well beyond the superficial, themed, retrofitting prevalent in suburban strip malls. Just as complexity makes the relationship between human and baboon both ironic yet beautiful, complexity must characterize the development of these architectural chimeras. As such, it rests clearly within the purview of the architect to assume control over professional destiny as well as that of the built environment. New technologies can enable architecture's segue back into the literal production and future of buildings.

NOTES

1. Mumford, Lewis. *The City in History: Its Origins, Its Transformations, Its Prospects.* New York: Harvest Books, 1968.
2. "Satellite Imaging of Narcotics Environmental Degredation." *U.S. Department of State International Information Program.* <usinfo.state.gov/products/pubs/andes/imaging.htm>
3. Whaley, Monte. "Neighborhood Pooper Snooper Acquitted," *Denver Post,* 19 July 2001.
4. Berkan, Riza and Trubatch, Sheldon. "Fuzzy Logic and Hybrid Approaches to Web Intelligence Gathering and Information Management." <suez.cs.gsu.edu/~cscyqz/research/wcci2002-cwi/Berkan.pdf>
5. Schoonmaker, Sara. "Trading On-Line: Information Flows in Advanced Capitalism." *The Information Society 9.1,* 1993.
6. Mies van der Rohe, "A Personal Statement by the Architect, 1964" in *Walter Blaser, Mies van der Rohe.* New York: Praeger Publishers, 1972.
7. "Industry Statistics," *Environmental Building News 10,* No. 5, May 2001.
8. "American Housing Survey for the United States: 2001", *U.S. Census Bureau, American Housing Survey Branch.* Washington, DC, 2002.
9. "Industry Statistics," *Environmental Building News 10,* No. 5, May 2001.
10. Zambito, Victoria. "Gehry and Guggenheim Reunite," *RedVector.com,* 30 July 2002.
11. Rosan, Richard M. "Real Estate Development Trends in the United States" President of the Urban Land Institute, in a speech given in Tokyo, Japan on December 11, 2002.
12. Thompson, D'Arcy. *On Growth and Form.* Cambridge: Cambridge University Press, 1992.
13. Robert J. Coen, Senior Vice President, Director of Forecasting at Universal McCann, made these predictions on July 10, 2002, to investment analysts and the business press at the University Club in New York City.
14. "United States Department of Commerce News", *U.S. Census Bureau, Economics and Statistics Administration.* Washington, DC. April 1, 2003.
15. Ibid. Rosan, Richard.
16. Paul Virilio, "From the Media Building to the Global City: New Scope for Contemporary Architecture and Urban Planning." *Crossings 1.1,* December 2000.

Beth Blostein is an assistant professor at the Knowlton School of Architecture at the Ohio State University. She received a B.S. in Architecture and an M.A. in Industrial Design from The Ohio State University, and she completed a Mater of Design Studies at Harvard University Graduate School of Design in 1996. Her work seeks to re-orient the practice of architecture by critically investigating the influence of new technologies on the conceptualization, realization, and ultimate reformulation of architecture. Recent awards include *Interactive Counterpoint* for the Art Interactive Design Competition, *Gradient House* for the Southeastern Center for Contemporary Art's HOME House Project, and *Casual Encounters* received first place in the *New Housing New York* Competition. She has exhibited at national and international venues, including the National Building Museum. Her research has been supported by the National Endowment for the Arts and the Battelle Endowment for Technology and Human Affairs.

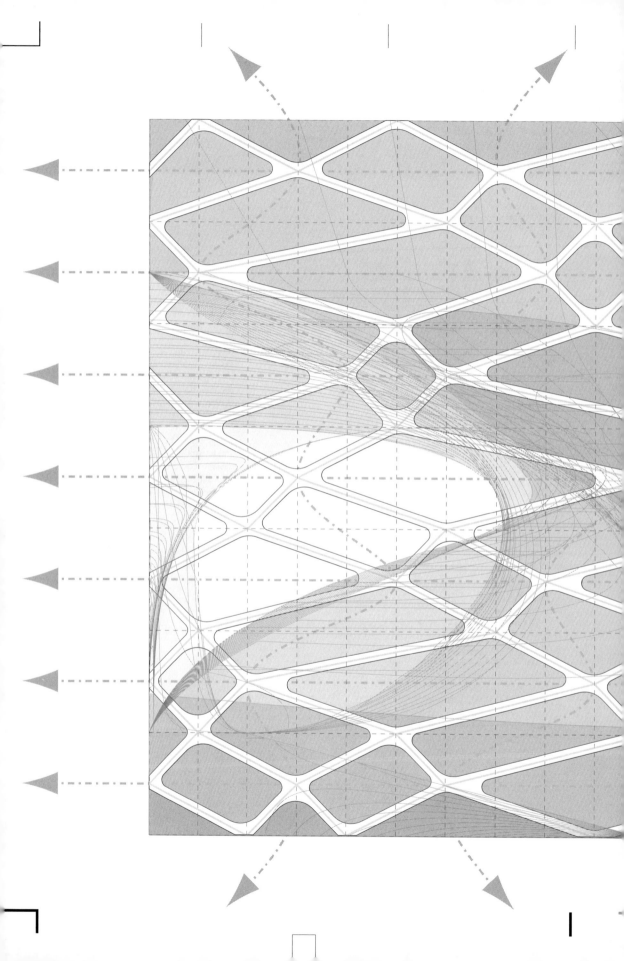

NAM JUNE PAIK MUSEUM

deixis in collaboration with Ingo Gunther

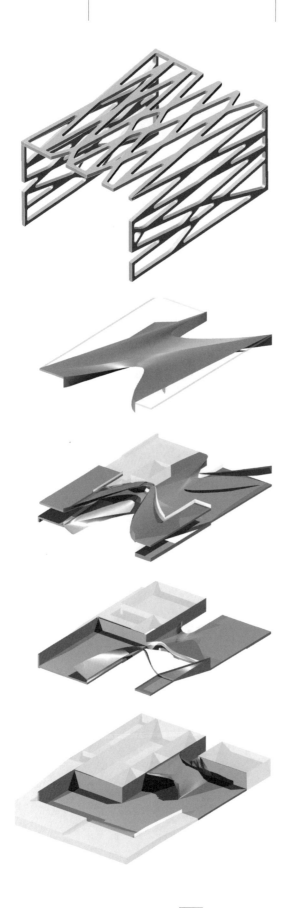

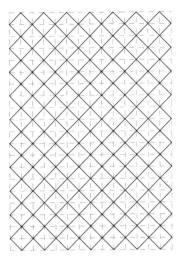

Normative modularity

Fluid viscosity

Science

Technology

Musician

Globalist

Normative modularity

Examining the range of artistic work created by multimedia pioneer Nam June Paik informed a specific approach to an architecture of transformation and adaptation. Though not designed as Paik might have, or with any desire to reconstruct the work of the artist in a different context or scale, the attitude toward the site, form and space takes inspiration from the artist. A fundamental preoccupation of Paik's was the desire to reach and interact with mass culture in a more immediate way than the visual arts had previously afforded. The utilization of the most pervasive and emerging medias: television, video, and broadcast technology provided an opportunity for a symbiotic relationship with the audience in which there was productive feedback into the system in the form of controlled interference. Like Paik's work, the architecture is imbedded in a particular context, yet through tactics of interference and disturbance emerges as something unpredictable. The emergence of the dynamic from of the static as a fluid condition — not juxtaposition — provides for the development of an extremely adaptable yet specific architecture.

The architecture of the museum takes its clues from many of the questions Paik asked through his work. Of particular importance are the seminal works that experimented with the effects of magnetic fields on cathode ray picture tubes found in early television sets. Paik's interest in the effects simple disturbances had on complex technology, and the resulting aesthetic and critical value that such disturbances might have greatly influenced the ordering of the building. A relatively rigid, cubic volume — normative museum/gallery typology — was transformed through a series of site and program driven disturbances leading to a condition in which conventionally controlled hermetic gallery space gives way to a responsive topologic interiority. This internal transformation of space allows for a radically different gallery environment that is now a variable and graduated condition.

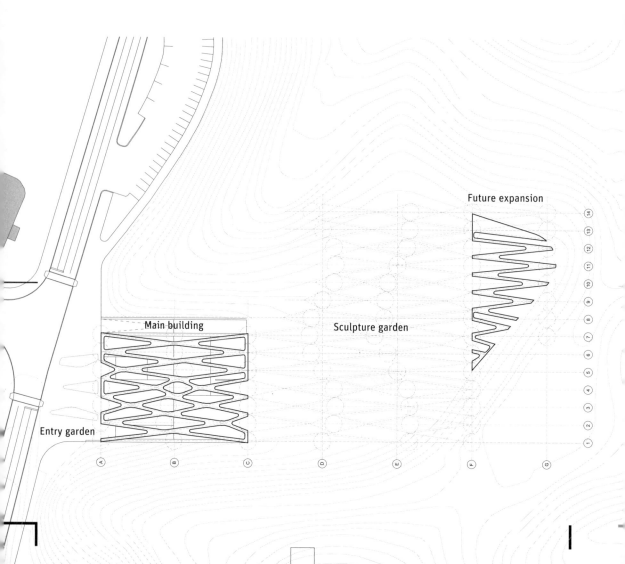

Future expansion

Main building

Sculpture garden

Entry garden

The gallery organization and sectional condition of the museum respond to both the steeply sloping site and the internal logic of the program. These soft interior spaces respond to many of Paik's traits — musician, technologist, scientist, globalist — while simultaneously providing a slippage with nature and site. The building *box* is situated in the low cleared area of the site, filling the small valley with an artificially measured plane, while the reciprocal condition — a flowing landscape of exhibition space, breaks out from the order of the box-envelope, leading directly to the sloped sculpture gardens and exterior exhibition spaces. The interior/exterior landscape measured against the datum of the enveloping weave creates a dynamic central organizing space that is more urban and information intensive in a manner that we believe to be at the soul of the work of Nam June Paik.

deixis is **Andrew Saunders, David Riebe, Ted Ngai,** and **Mark Mistur** — an architectural practice actively involved in design and research. The partners' involvement in both practice and academic institutions affords the opportunity for ongoing built and un-built architectural research. The utilization of emerging technologies and materials in developing systemic, adaptive and responsive built environments is central to their investigations. The Nam June Paik Museum Competition published here was done in collaboration with the artist Ingo Gunther, and with Katalina Arboleda, Josef Fuentes and Patrick Wong.

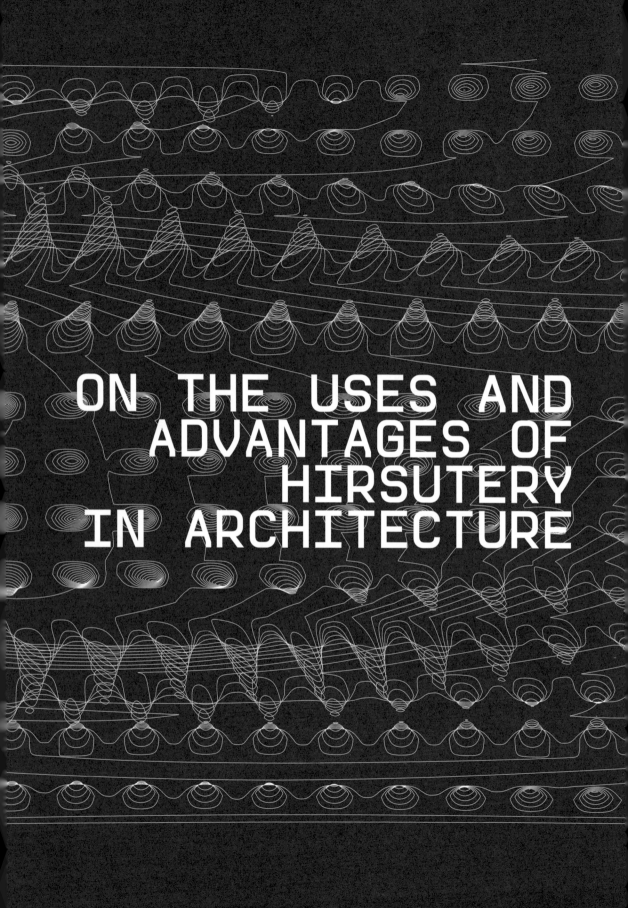

ON THE USES AND ADVANTAGES OF HIRSUTERY IN ARCHITECTURE

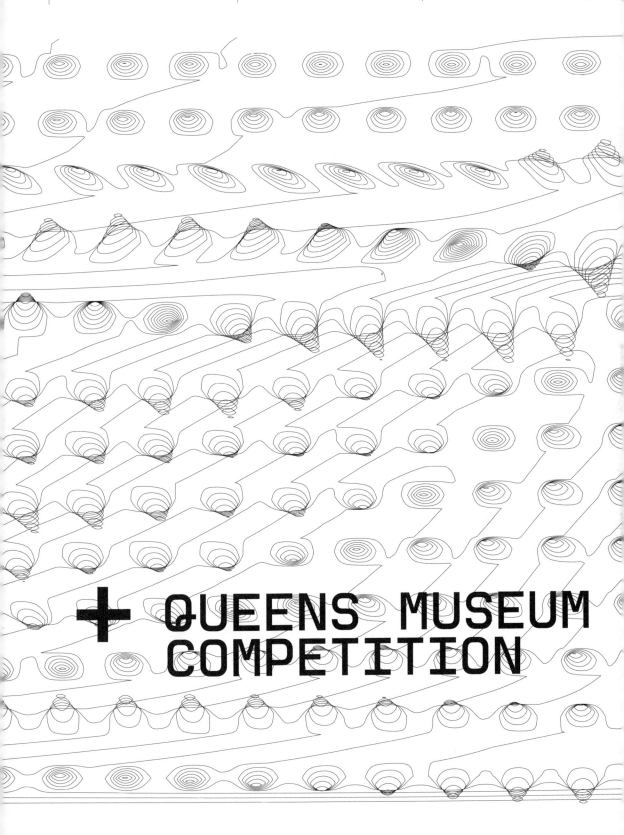

+ QUEENS MUSEUM COMPETITION

gnuform : Jason Payne and Heather Roberge

ON THE USES AND ADVANTAGES OF HIRSUTERY IN ARCHITECTURE

Hirsutery

Beyond the world of surfaces and sheets lies a class of materiality more aligned with hairlike structures and branching systems. Inherent to these is a stickiness and thickness that we are drawn to, one that resists the slippery transparency of surfaces — especially digital ones — by virtue of geometry: hair tangles and mats, branches fork and interlock, strands weave and comb through one another. These organizations of material come loaded with the basic mechanics for the development of unusual techniques and the production of underexploited structures and sensibilities. Working with these types of material involves the generation of many small yet carefully-designed connections between very delicate structures. These gradually build up to produce patterns and rhythms that are often highly detailed and of a fullness which might be capable of handling architecturally-scaled masses and volumes.

These are *material* systems. Line-based systems in architecture — grids, paths, courses, contours, boundaries, etc. — have often understood organization to come first, materialization second. In this view, an organization makes some particular material implementation possible, with *line* being affiliated with the former and *volume* and *form* associated with the latter. This might be due to the nature of lines: they are not physical, as they are understood in their pure sense to have no thickness. Branches, too, have been understood as organizational elements, probably because of their cursory resemblance to lines. Geometrically speaking, however, branches, hairs, and trajectories might be understood as tubes: long, thin surfaces wrapped around and upon themselves. This characteristic makes them useful first as matter, then as organization, making the production of emergent form and order possible. These systems are models of material behavior, not organizational layout.

Some Observations on Hairlike Structures and Branching Systems

They produce furry bodies. When used as material that is behaving as opposed to fields of behavior, these systems produce what might be called near-objects. If grown properly, they congeal into bodies that have distinct yet highly involute boundaries, which gives them their fuzzy appearance. Often their edge is not a thin skin but rather a thickened

zone, a zone filled with material rather than an empty area. They also contain defined structures at various scales with differing characteristics, and their boundaries tend to be fuzzy as well. As a result of the delicacy of any individual element — hair, branch, etc. — they do not harden. Further, this variegated outer zone takes the *outer* environment in to such a degree that the structure becomes thoroughly immersed within it, lending greater complexity to dichotomies such as inside-outside and context-organism. Mats, hairballs, bundles, and the like are all such objects, existing somewhere between inert forms and fluctuating fields.

In recent years much work has been invested in the production of architecture using a model of morphogenesis developed largely by d'Arcy Thompson, a model which conceives of growth as the generator of form: ". . .the form of an organism is determined by its rate of growth in various directions." This model has proven to be highly productive of new form in architecture and will undoubtedly continue to be so. There is an alternative model, however, which operates somewhat differently from that of Thompson but which nevertheless deals with the behavior of matter; for this reason it should be understood in paradigmatic conjunction with the Thompson model. In certain cases the two may even be deployed together to form a kind of strategic interaction. In Thompson's model, morphogenesis concerns an organism in which ". . .material is introduced into the organism and transferred from one part of it to another," The second, alternative model involves the flow of matter through an environment, a flow which, while highly organized as a discrete entity, never entirely consumes its surrounding material. Always suspended within its medium, flows never resolve into disconnected bodies. This second model finds its origins in Alan Turing's work on reaction-diffusion processes in which "the systems considered consist of masses of tissues which are not growing, but within which certain substances are reacting chemically, and through which they are diffusing. These substances are called morphogens, the word being intended to convey the idea of a form producer." The production of architecture within a model such as this produces a methodological framework in which primary attention is given to the saturation of structures within environments and thus, the production of atmosphere.

They make it possible to move beyond the problem of the inflected surface. Conventionally defined, single surfaces seem to need foreign material and external constraints to provide their inflection and ultimate form. There is nothing wrong with this, and in fact strategies of surfaces wrapped up in their contexts — and vice-versa

— will undoubtedly always be productive. However, the production of a furry materiality leads down a distinctly different avenue in terms of both methodology and morphology —methodologically, because we have inverted the material/organizational relationship, and morphologically, because very strange forms emerge that challenge received notions of architectural enclosure, structure, and use. Branching systems are embedded with their own internal rules for growth, providing the basis for their unfolding form. This independence from external forces — at least at first — affords them an initial material fullness that single surfaces don't have.

In this series of images we observe the fusion of two initially separate branches. The two are geometrically similar, though not the same, in their initial design. Near symmetries tend to produce material arrangements conducive to structured integration, allowing for various *fits* to occur — combing, weaving, braiding, etc. — while maintaining just enough dissimilarity to roughen the edges, enabling cohesion between elements. At a certain point in its growth cycle, the primary strands break into a secondary, more delicately scaled system which is also nearly symmetrical. These begin to interlock, slowing growth and producing a large webbed structure containing internal fronts that move inward before dispersing.

They proliferate wildly. These kinds of systems grow exponentially. Branches sprout new branches, hairs split into more strands, tangles become increasingly matted. As more material is produced, more interactions occur, spurring continual jumps in production. If single surfaces have too little materiality, hairy systems sometimes have too much. Sometimes they have to be trimmed, and sometimes they produce mats so dense that they don't work at all. This series of images shows a set of branches proliferating all the more quickly due to their containment. Their forced close proximity creates an ever-increasing rate of production until individual strands begin to blend and meld into a kind of slowly undulating, heavy cloud. It is at this point that larger structures become visible.

Structurally, they produce stiffness rather than hardness. Hairs bend and clump instead of breaking and crumbling. Piles are resilient and continuous, not brittle and fragmented. These properties are especially apparent as material pushes against more material or against an external constraint. This is true not only of individual strands, but also of the larger structures that emerge as they pile up. This characteristic allows these organizations to withstand and even feed off of external pressures — the constriction of boundaries in the case of the experiments shown

here — transferring these forces into some interior structure.

They expand inward. Hairs are tubes, and tubes are surfaces, so as a branching system grows it produces more and more surface. Due to the often curled, intertwined nature of this extension, an unusual type of expanse is often produced - one that moves inward as opposed to outward. In light of this, the customary understanding of architectural vastness — as broad, empty space extending outward — needs redefinition to include both extension inward and material fullness. In the structure shown, a brief period of initial growth establishes the strands that form fixed boundaries, at which time all further growth shifts to the two very dense interior ridges. Strands in this region intertwine to form swirled fronts that shift as a whole. This movement creates the waves visible moving out across the exterior strands.

They dismantle the conventional hierarchy of architectural scales. Historically, architectural magnitude has been understood to exist across five categories of scale: regional, urban, architectural, interior, and furniture. While it would seem that these scales would cover any size organization or form an architect might work with, in reality it tends to relegate material into five conceptual headings wholly inadequate for the description of the real behavior of matter in space and time. Just as the terms red, green and blue cannot begin to describe the infinite number of hues in the world, so too does a vertical hierarchy of just five scales fail to represent the variegations of size in architecture. Of course, designers realize that multiple scales exist between these five, but their existence as categorical benchmarks tends to give them an operational importance in the process of design that then precludes these other *in-between* scales from asserting their possible priority in morphogenesis. Particle flows resist easy scalar categorization into previously established ideals, and instead agglomerate into magnitudes particular to their internal design and external environment. Working with particle animations allows an initial avoidance of generalizing scalar conventions, enabling the production of very specific — much more specific than a category would provide — scales of matter and organization.

These unique scales then allow for the creation of new hierarchies, each one particular to the project at hand.

> ...That was weird...
> —Driver to passenger in a recent
> Volkswagen commercial

At a recent conference on the possible urbanisms for New York City's East River edge, Jeff Kipnis began a talk by showing a video of a Volkswagen commercial in which a young couple drive slowly down a rainy New Orleans street, startled to find the music from the car stereo gradually synchronizing with the rhythms of the windshield wipers and various activities occurring on the sidewalk. Researchers involved in complexity studies know this phenomenon as entrainment: the seemingly spontaneous ability of disparate elements to come together into a larger, coherent pattern. Just as significantly, the bemused occupants of the VW know it as "weird." Kipnis understood it as proof of the broad, cultural emergence of a kind of sensibility of "rhythmicity," a sensibility shared now by everyone from the television-viewing public to the scientists of complexity, from Madison Avenue advertisers to architectural designers. The use of particle animation during the design process for the production of hairy structures allows us to tap into this rhythmicity, which is very much an effect of real flows of matter in space and time. We hope that the products of this sort of rhythmic morphogenesis enhance and intensify the pulsating atmosphere that surrounds us. Thus far we have found particle flows and the mats, hairballs, bundles, and other material they produce to be rather unruly, both in terms of their resistance to architectural convention as well as their continually changing configurations. This makes taming these flows into architecturally recognizable organizations difficult, but it is within this difficulty that lies their promise, as matter is forced far from the equilibrium of convention.

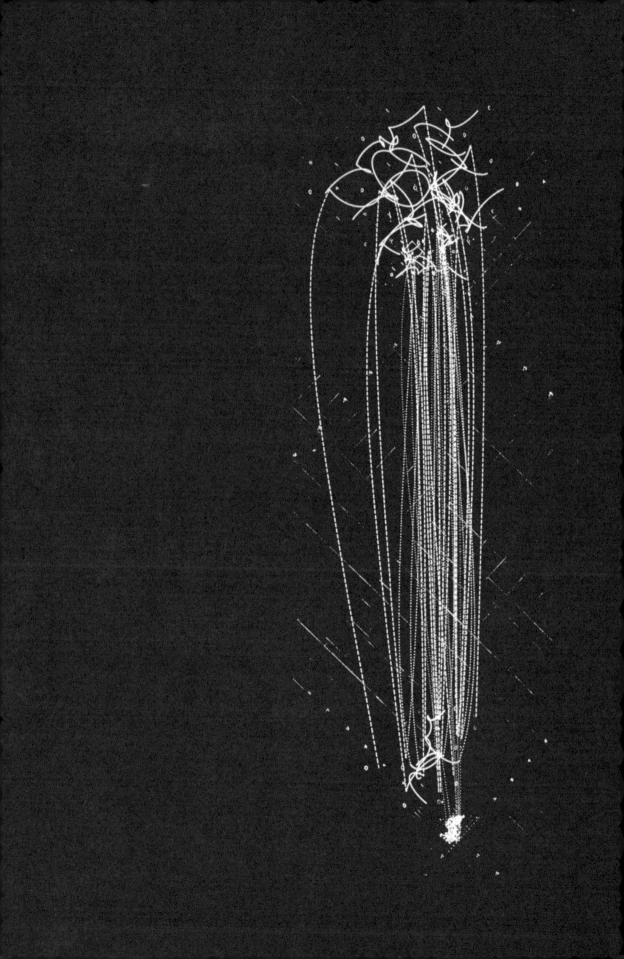

QUEENS MUSEUM EXPANSION COMPETITION

> Rhythm is originally the rhythm of the feet.
> —Elias Canetti

Our strategy for the physical and conceptual expansion of the Queens Museum of Art shapes the Museum's future as a leading institution for the exhibition of emerging and alternative forms of art and performance. In concert with this, our scheme provides an extensive infrastructure to promote various forms of public assembly. We propose a complex within the existing envelope comprised of a layered set of structures — the spaces and surfaces of which amplify and express the dynamics inherent within large groups of people. In this way, the Museum's infrastructure will draw upon the patterns, rhythms, and formations generated through crowd behavior to create visible yet transitory structures within and around those of the built environment. Exhibition, then, becomes an activity immersed within a larger, more variegated field of intensified public gathering. Moreover, the overt physicality of the infrastructure we propose requires that the exhibition and consumption of art move beyond the standard confines of cerebral interpretation and into the realm of the body. This seems appropriate given the increasingly dynamic atmospheres created with new forms of artistic expression. In a sense, the appreciation of art has always been about the experiencing of surface, and the evolution of art has largely been a matter of the extension and changing complexions of its surfaces. Our scheme promotes the expansion of these surfaces into and through those of the museum, the same surfaces across which an increasingly engaged spectator moves.

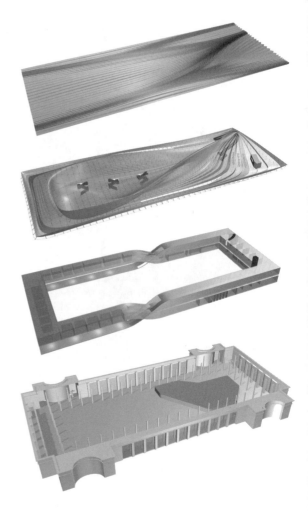

PLEATED ROOF— A new roof extends to edges of existing envelope, unifying old and new and strengthening existing building proportions. Pleat pattern resonates with rhythms of multi-purpose surface and suspension net, producing a thickened visual atmosphere. Changing density of translucent pleats creates differentiated lighting conditions on surface below.

LIVE SURFACE— Multi-purpose stepped surface provokes various patterns of public occupation and movement in conjunction with structured and unstructured events occurring upon it. Crowd formations become events unto themselves.

PERIPHERAL GALLERIES— Inserted within the existing envelope and structural system, two stacked peripheral volumes contain long term programs requiring fixed organization. Functions include permanent collections and exhibits having standard *white box* formatting and display requirements.

EXISTING BUILDING— Existing footprint, envelope and structural system is retained. Current roof over double-high volume is removed to provide room for new pleated surface and roof. Existing dividing wall on ground level is removed, providing a large, flexible central space to accommodate temporary exhibitions and less structured events. The underside of the live surface overhead generates internal unity and sectional intensification — a cloud formation above the main volume and Panorama.

Live Surfaces

Sloped and stepped surfaces have long been used in architecture and urbanism to modulate the flow of bodies through space. These devices imbue spatial experience with overt, even muscular, physicality. This thickening of the physiological atmosphere is often critical to the successful design and planning of public spaces and institutions. Among the most dynamic civic spaces in New York City are the entry to the Metropolitan Museum of Art and the open fields of Central Park. With this observation as a point of departure, our approach to the reconfiguration of Queens Museum involves the implementation of a large, pleated surface designed for a variety of different types of occupation.

The variegated surface is slung from the existing structural system — augmented as necessary — and supported by a suspension net. The surface is both vast and variegated, qualities required for the generation of an effective exteriority within the Museum. In a very real sense, this structure draws sensibilities and behaviors typically associated with exteriority into the building. This live surface produces an environment that, in places, is free of the confining associations attached to the modern white box and other forms of standard exhibition. The freedom of this internalized exteriority lies in its ability to tap into the resonance between the fluctuating rhythms of crowd formations and the increasingly dynamic atmospheres created with new forms of art, performance, and event.

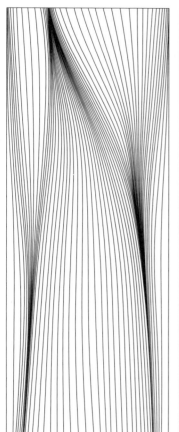

Gnuform

Jason Payne received his Master of Science in Advanced Architectural Design from Columbia University and his Bachelor of Architecture from SCI-Arc. He has taught at SCI-Arc, Bennington College, Rensselear Polytechnic Institute, Pratt Institute, Rice University and most recently at the University of California Los Angeles. He has also been involved in several award winning projects in association with Reiser+Umemoto Architects / RUR and Daniel Libeskind Architects.

Heather Roberge received her Master of Architecture from The Ohio State University. She has taught at Rensselear Polytechnic Institute, Pratt Institute and most recently University of California Los Angelese. Heather has been involved in award winning projects at both Eisenman Architects and Architecture Research Office.

Jason and Heather have lectured extensively throughout the United States and Europe. Their work has been published and exhibited throughout the United States, Japan, Slovakia and Korea. On exhibit in 2004 at the University of California Los Angeles Perloff Gallery is *GNUFORM: HAIRSTYLE.* They founded Gnuform in 1999.

Rhythmic Correlation

The organizational lines of the roof, stepped surface, and structural suspension net resonate visually and experientially. This rhythmic correlation between elements generates shifting specificities within the spaces of the building, activating its surfaces. Layered synchronicities work to blend and blur the distinctions between art objects and events, the exhibition infrastructure in place to display them, and the Museum visitors themselves. The same structures that modulate the movement of people also affect artistic expression, invigorating and extending the acts of exhibition and observation.

Part of the problem of the *white box* as applied to museum design is more fundamental than that of its privileging certain forms and periods of art over others. Aside from these affiliations, the white box has also come to symbolize solitary reflection and passive consumption of art, promoting a kind of alienation of the individual from the very masses the museum seeks to collect. It is possible and, in fact, necessary to avoid this form of alienated collectivity in favor of more open and dynamic forms of public gathering. Changing cultural sensibilities, more diverse museum-going demographics, and new forms of art and performance demand a built environment that integrates and amplifies the physical and social relations between people.

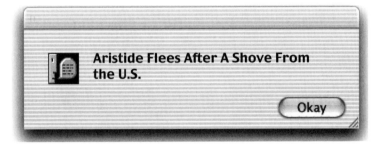

THE INVISIBLES[1]

Biot(h)ing : Alisa Andrasek

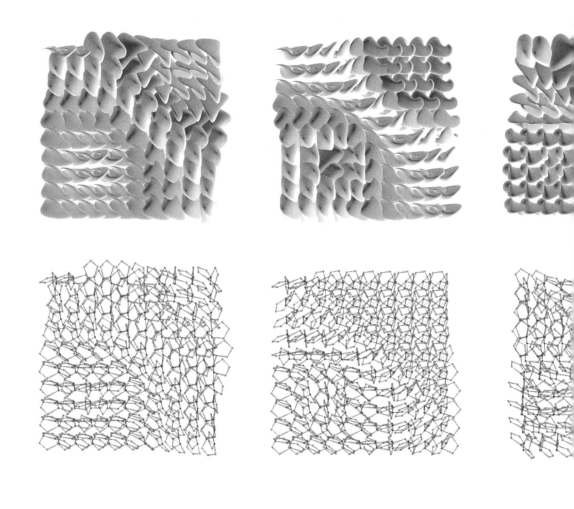

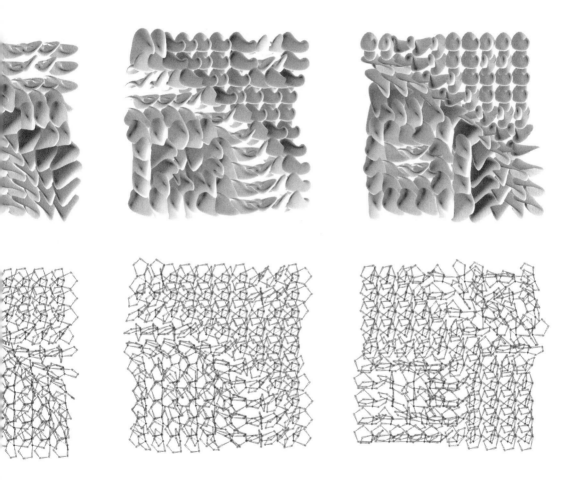

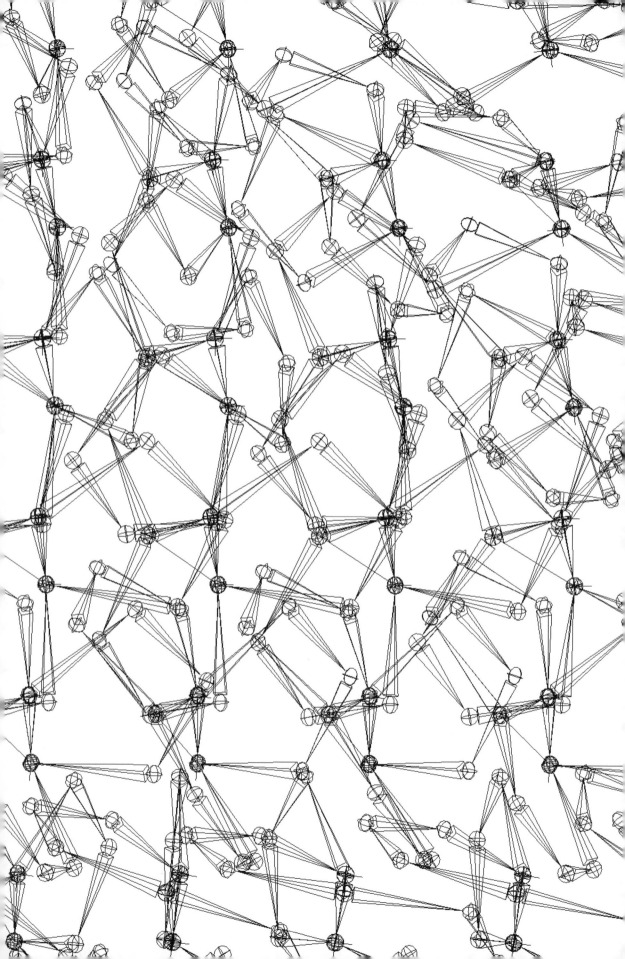

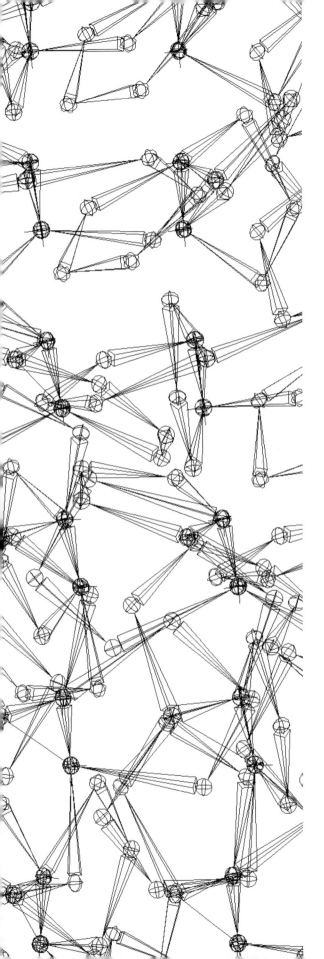

Molecular Revolutions[2]

Somewhere between the contemporary phenomenon of the smart mob (improvisational on-line communities organized along P2P networks) and the smart cloud (autopoetic environments driven by nanotechnology), biot(h)ing imagines a future at drift, indeterminately configured by the presence of another intelligence — invisible and ever-present. . .immanent and immense. . .No longer the static manifolds of an industrial age, this century's architecture is a smart architecture.

Fundamental drifting of existing presets is rooted in the multiplications of new kinds of uncontainable intelligence. New paradigms of power and control are exercised through the logics of molecular intelligence and its emerging new forms: molecular revolutions, biopolitics, mutant identities, fuzzy logics. . .These biot(h)ings are new forms of life, replicating themselves through various host milieus. They are emerging as singularities, away from individuations as subject or form.

It is the presence of collective autocatalysis within current molecular cultures, in its fictional and non-fictional, material and immaterial states, which presents to us an entirely new perception of environment. . .one less formal, less spatial, defined not by the conventions of boundary and border or by the presence of what we understand to be visible space, but by the atmospheric, the strangely physical, and yet not — event atmospheres . . . a translogical mist through which new architectures of latent political power synchronically emerge and dissolve. . .a kind of cultural weather system in constant flux and formation. Design enters a new form of incorporeality, which embeds transient behaviors with, and mutations within its matter. . .

Extreme Materiality

This project imagines a new kind of materiality — the precedent of another intelligence — one in the making . . . It is developing post-software instrumentalities in which matter and information are converging into a new kind of substance — embodied autopoesis . . . The invisibles work with material micropolitics, zooming into ubiquitous microstructures that blur the boundary between code and material. It is engendering new posthuman occurrences, ones that recall the ambiguity of quantum levels, whose weirdness is somehow mirrored in the *otherness* of a post-gender mutant population, biology as genetic coding, quantum cryptography . . . Its identities are polymorphic probabilities . . . It starts in the middle, at the level of the molecular. Every particle incorporates perpetual movement. The scalable relationships of velocities of elastic particles are genetic information that propagates through the

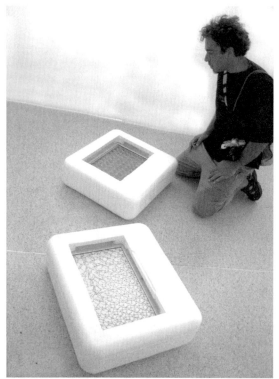

Installation for the exhibition *Aion: An Eventual Architecture* curated by
Andrea Di Stefano at the 2003 Prague Biennale

system. Variant intensities aggregate and engender different field conditions, if substance is to be understood as a coalescence of material — an immanent plane that exceeds itself through its polymorphic transformations.[3]

Translogics

> . . . If architecture pursues extending diagrams into biograms it will become more what it has always been: a materialist art of qualitative body modulation, a translogical engineering of matter gone mindful. . .
>
> —Brian Massumi[4]

This project works translogically in its interlacing of multiple software environments. It could be understood as a form of artificial synesthesia through the actions of its layers that are inextricably affected by each other. They are rematerializing the invisible substance through the expressive becoming of it's extreme materiality.

Connective tissue is formed through mathematical relationships as a medium of exchange between different axiomatic infrastructures. Patterns of material organization emerge when functions run through different environments, affecting their discreet agents. Agents come in the forms of sound molecules, non-linear equations of time, and morphogenetics, and they accumulate in various host conditions.

The nature of their intricate relationship is inscribed in algorithms, which unravel through emergent patterns of a new kind of nature. The relationship of the layers is not through a sequence of translation from one media to another in a cause-effect way, but rather through the simultaneity of events that spread via the infinite line of aion.[5]

Intrinsic to the logics of this project is an investigation of the potential forms of interface of seemingly incompatible software from various disciplinary origins. It propagates a post-software future, one in which information becomes a form of life, pure intelligent substance, moving seamlessly from one environment to another. It also promotes a post-disciplinary future, where insights of different expertise converge.

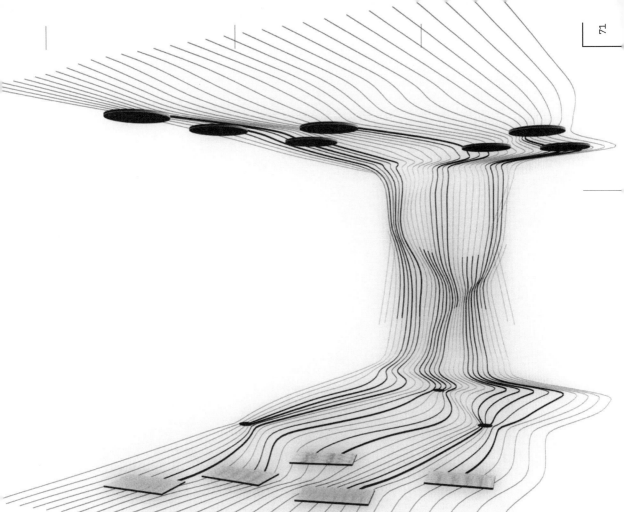

Installation diagram

The core of this synesthetic hinge is Max MSP, an interactive sound programming environment that alters conventional forms of musical composition through the incorporation of algorithmically based processes. The user navigates the software's internal intelligence less like a composer and more like a programmer, adjusting various parameters to indirectly influence the system's internal network dynamics. Mutations emerge when the system is triggered by the input of various sensors. A current pattern runs back through the process and simultaneously forward to the formation of a new pattern.

Cellular Polymorphism

Maya Embedded Language (MEL) is used as an autopoetic infrastructure for generating cellular polymorphic membranes. Transitional activators are programmed into a ubiquitous field of skeletal cells and through progressive differentiation define a zone of influence. The speed of rotation is derived from a weighted average based on the speed of each of the three transitional activators. The hierarchy of influence is acknowledged in the diagram by different line weights. The heaviest connects the cell to the activator with the most influence, while the lightest line joins the cell to the point with the least influence over its speed.

Closest to the attractor, a zone of fusion and corresponded inflection is indexed in each individual cell. Cellular skin inflection is the emergent property of the active relationship of the skin and its correspondent skeletal cell. The circulation of data within the system generates excess value and breeds itself through always new incarnations. Dynamic morphologies have intrinsic long-term tendencies but at the same time are passing through continual modulation and an irreducible self-difference of the field events. Since the frequencies of recurrent topological features are modified through endogenous transformations of the syn(es)thetic layer, they drift and propagate non-pulsating time.

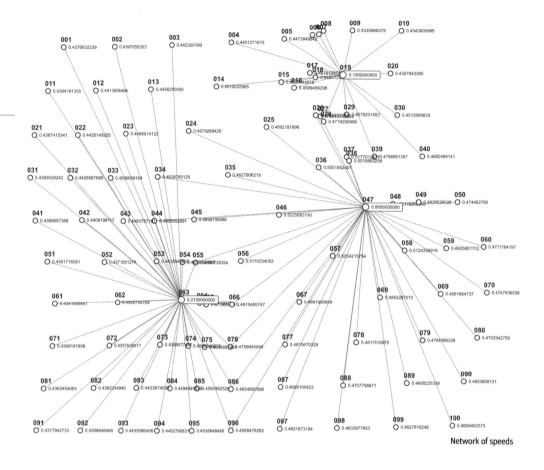

Network of speeds

Sonorous Landscapes

All sound is an integration of grains, of elementary sonic particles, of sonic quanta.
—Xenakis[6]

. . . We should say, rather, that territorial motifsform rhythmic faces or characters, and that territorial counterpoints form melodic landscapes. . .the melodic landscape is no longer a melody associated with a landscape; the melody itself is a sonorous landscape in counterpoint to a virtual landscape. . .
—Deleuze and Guattari[7]

Aural sense is one of becoming-molecular in music. Instead of pure notes, molecules of sound are scripted through a process of granular synthesis. The granular synthesis of sound is the generation of thousands of short sonic grains which are combined linearly to form large-scale audio events. The characteristics of the grains are definable and these combine to give the nature of the overall sound. Sonar molecules, as well as their durational relationships, are understood through the logics of materiality and non-pulsating time.[8] The patterns inherent to a code are rendered audible through the interactions of a population of molecular oscillators. The invisible life force of another kind of nature is materialized into an aural landscape. Counterintuitive effects structured through non-pulsating time become perceptible. Sound patterns are projected into space through a holosonic[9] interface. One passes the field encountering different vibrations of sonar projections. Sound is self-breeding into space, its drifting frequencies modulate one's experience, zooming in and out through the sonic grains. . .

Parametric distribution of average speeds

#	speed	#	speed	#	speed	#	speed	#	speed	#	speed	#	speed	#	speed	#	speed	#	speed
1	.4377	2	.4397	3	.4423	4	.4451	5	.4474	6	.4478	7	.4449	8	.4389	9	.4336	10	.4344
11	.4384	12	.4414	13	.4456	14	.4510	15	.4565	16	.4599	17	.4579	18	.4485	19	.1500	20	.4388
21	.4387	22	.4426	23	.4507	24	.4639	25	.4828	26	.5052	27	.5177	28	.5019	29	.4799	30	.4652
31	.4383	32	.4427	33	.4423	34	.4451	35	.4474	36	.4478	37	.4449	38	.4389	39	.4336	40	.4344
41	.4370	42	.4408	43	.4494	44	.4655	45	.4900	46	.5226	47	.9500	48	.5219	49	.4926	50	.4745
51	.4351	52	.4372	53	.4439	54	.4609	55	.4851	56	.5110	57	.5254	58	.4352	59	.4372	60	.4438
61	.4342	62	.4343	63	.2100	64	.4539	65	.4739	66	.4910	67	.4992	68	.4953	69	.4852	70	.4748
71	.4348	72	.4358	73	.4399	74	.4508	75	.4644	76	.4757	77	.4816	78	.4812	79	.4764	80	.4703
81	.4363	82	.4382	83	.4424	84	.4495	85	.4580	86	.4655	87	.4699	88	.4708	89	.4688	90	.4654
91	.4378	92	.4399	93	.4434	94	.4483	95	.4539	96	.4588	97	.4622	98	.4634	99	.4628	100	.4609

Non-Sense (Through the Looking Glass)

> . . . When forces become necessarily cosmic,
> material becomes necessarily molecular, with
> enormous force
> operating in an infinitesimal space. . .
> —Deleuze and Guattari[10]

This project occupies the non-sensical, the territory of Alice.[11] In Alice's world, realities are generated through language. Snark is neither snake nor shark — but a product of imagination fabricated through words. The fast reality of the White Rabbit and the slippery polymorphic passage of Alice both acquire their shapes on the surface of speech.[12] Alice climbs to the surface, out of the constraints of false depth. She ventures into becoming unlimited, into possible worlds instead of the earth's underground. Her landscape is a topological fiction; her weather is horizontal mist . . .incorporeal intelligence. Carroll constructs the game of non-sense, the ideal game in which rules need to be invented. In order to play this game, one needs to immerse into the polymorphic territory of the game, embrace the unprecedented, go beyond the limits of meaning and signs. "In which way, in which way?" asks Alice, feeling that it is always in both ways at the same time. This *becoming* happens along the neutral, infinite line of pure event. On the plane of immanence things vary in dimension and they become bigger and smaller at the same time. Through the instruments of computation one could set up a different kind of physics. Weirdness occurring through the counterintuitive effects one experiences in the aural field of *The Invisibles* is a product of new intelligence populating the fabric of space. Counterintuitive physics are set up through an axiomatic infrastructure. It is software, instrumental and spatial, design as genetic inscription, which we are engineering. A minuscule coding change could send a powerful rupture through the system. The parallel reality of the invisible code is a common ground for multiple actualizations. Intelligence systems, interiority of which is time, extend beyond a singular scale.

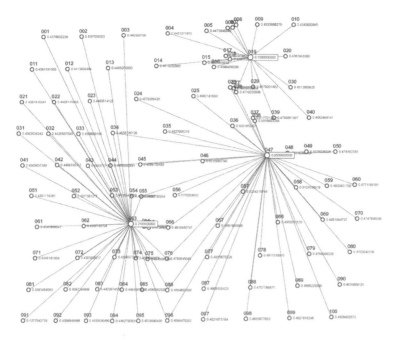
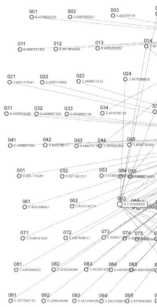

Intrinsic to the logics of the project is a multiscalar condition. The game of nonsense is on.[13]

> . . . In music, it's no longer a matter of an absolute ear but rather an impossible ear that can alight on someone, arise briefly in someone . . .
>
> —Gilles Deleuze[14]

Time is not a measurement line any more — it is understood as a material that can be molded, stretched, compressed. . .it is scripted. It extends over the infinite line of aion.

Dynamic blueprints transfiltrate ambient intelligence as it is incarnated through a multitude of entangled layers. The syn(es)thetic branches of this aural creature are subject to cumulative changes triggered by logics of interlinked transformational filters and the system's own axiomatic infrastructures.

In the perpetual movement of its durational molecules, the fibers of the connective tissue frequently drift out of phase to discover ever new territories. . .This procedural life form mutates its host milieu through an array of counterintuitive sensorial effects — as an ephemeral, ever changing, fantasy-expanding environment.

This ghostly alien alters its environmental conditions at exaggerated speeds. Its identity structures are not singular but multiple. It propagates non-pulsating time through its mediated processes. The creative potential of aion unravels through the breeding of sonic drizzles — affective constellations of sonar molecules; a resonating hive which disrupts its host's reverberations. . . The invisible structures are emitted and become actualized into a world of matter — heterogeneous but coherent streams of invisible data, newly visible, and yet invisible.

Alisa Andrasek is an experimental practitioner of architecture and computational processes in design. In 2001 she founded biot(h)ing, a multidisciplinary laboratory whose research focuses on the translogical and generative potential of physical and artificial computational systems for design. Andrasek graduated from the School of Architecture, University of Zagreb and holds a Masters in Advanced Architectural Design from Columbia University. She teaches at both Columbia University and the University of Pennsylvania and has also taught at Rensselaer Polytechnic Institute and Pratt Institute.

biot(h)ing — Alisa Andrasek, Gabriel Bach, Andrea Flamenco, Kevin Kane, Adam Marcus and Michael Rabinovich

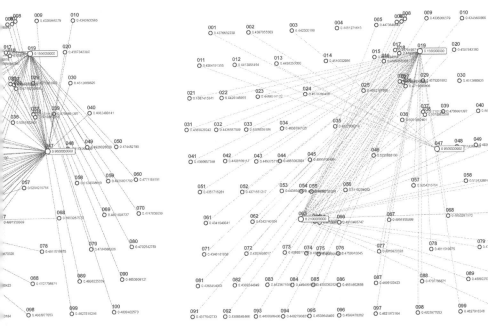

Variations on a network of speed.

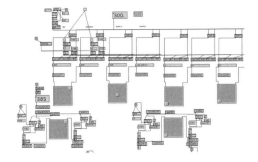

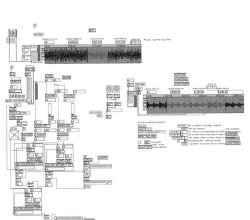

Captures of Max/MSP interface

NOTES

1. Bergson, Henri. *Matter and Memory*, Trans. Nancy Margaret Paul and W. Scott Palmer, Zone Books.
2. Borges, J. L. *Labyrinths*, A New Directions Book, 1964.
3. Massumi, Brian. *Parables for the Virtual: Movement, Affect, Sensation (Post-Contemporary Interventions)*, Duke University Press, 2002.
4. Ibid. Massumi, Brian.
5. Ibid. Borges.
6. Xenakis, Iannis. *Formalized Music; Thought And Mathematics In Composition*, Bloomington: Indiana University Press, 1971.
7. Deleuze, Gillies and Felix Guattari. "Of the Refrain," *A Thousand Plateaus: Capitalism and Schizophrenia*, Trans. Brian Massumi, Minneapolis: University of Minnesota Press, 1987.
8. Deleuze, Gilles. Conference Presentation on Musical Time, IRCAM.
9. Holosonic Research Labs. <http://www.holosonics.com> 2004.
10. Ibid, Deleuze and Guattari.
11. Carroll, Lewis. *Alice in Wonderland*, New York: W.W. Norton & Co., 1992.
12. Carroll, Lewis. "Plain Superficiality is the character of speech. . ." *The Dynamics of a Particle* (Collected Works of Lewis Carroll), Classic Books, 2000.
13. Ibid. Carroll. *Alice in Wonderland*.
14. Ibid. Deleuze.

BEDFORD AVENUE - BROOKLYN - NY

Bettina Johae

Bettina Johae, Dipl. Ing. Architecture, MA Studio Art, studied architecture and art at the Technical University Berlin; the Illinois Institute of Technology, Chicago; Columbia College, Chicago; New York University. She holds a Master in Architecture from the TU Berlin and a Master in Studio Art from NYU.

She is the recipient of several grants and awards, including a scholarship from the German Academic Exchange Service (DAAD) and student excellence awards from NYU and the TU Berlin. Her works about urban environments in transition have been shown in several exhibitions. She also works as an independent curator.

Raised in Berlin, she has lived in Brooklyn, NY since 2001.

Carola Ebert, Dipl. Ing. Architect MSc, architect and critic, runs a small practice for residential projects in Berlin, Germany. She has been a visiting critic and lecturer at various universities in Berlin and London and has presented her research on Composite Practices in Architecture, the 1960s, and Architectural Ideologies at various conferences in Europe. She studied architecture at the Technical University Berlin and The Bartlett, University College London and holds a Master in Architecture from the TU Berlin and a Master of Science in Architectural History and Theory from The Barlett, UCL.

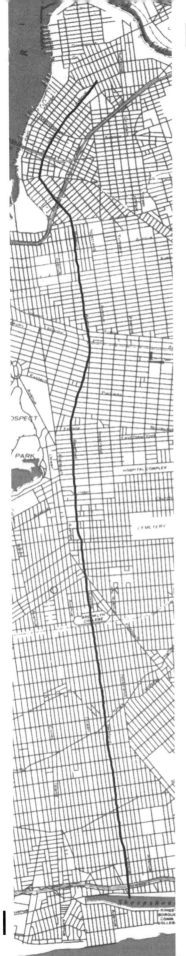

Bettina Johae's project *bedford avenue* examines Brooklyn, NY, along its longest north-south street. A video recording shot from her bicycle explores the full length of Bedford Avenue from Greenpoint in the north to Sheepshead Bay, its southern end at the waterfront. The complete traversal exposes Bedford Avenue's diverse and sometimes drastically-changing character. While for many contemporary hipsters Bedford Avenue consists of only a few blocks around the Bedford Avenue subway station, *bedford avenue — brooklyn — ny* explores the entire street and its different connotations: The residence of the Hasidic Rabbi, remnants of Bedford-Stuyvesant's roughest times, barred up storefronts next to church after church, well-kept detached picket-fenced houses near Sheepshead Bay.

The original installation, first shown in 2002 at Modern Culture at The Gershwin Hotel, New York, consists of two videos, a map of Bedford Avenue, a text listing all intersecting street names, and a series of color photographs — 19 stills taken from the video screen. The two videos show the complete sequence of Bedford Avenue's eastern and western elevation respectively, dissecting Brooklyn and its neighborhoods: from the hip areas in northern Williamsburg, through an ultra-orthodox Jewish community and some rougher urban spots, to the leafy residential suburbs in the south, often separated only by an intersection. The combination of the footage of the two rides along Bedford Avenue with selected c-prints feeds on the subtle friction between the different media. While the videos offer an unedited view of the succession of the different areas, the exhibited stills show the artist's choice of what she considers their main characteristics. Individually, some stills seem to affirm traditional portraits of Brooklyn as Manhattan's rougher *underground* sister, while others contradict these with pleasant views of charming houses, front lawns and wooden fences. Viewed as an ensemble, the stills highlight Bettina Johae's emphasis on the cuts and frictions between a variety of independent and incongruous neighborhoods along Bedford Avenue.

By exhibiting a variety of media Bettina Johae emphasizes the limitations and specific subjectivity of each of them: the seemingly realistic version of Bedford Avenue in the videos — a ride down the street at just one certain day; the conventions and abstractions of a map, the evocative and repetitive list of crossroads. Her artistic interpretation in the c-prints with their saturated hue and pattern of blurry stripes — remnants of the video screen — suggest yet another Bedford Avenue; intense but secretive, colorful but somehow frozen just before or after something happened. In doing so, the installation as a whole doesn't aim to assign a new meaning to Bedford Avenue. Instead, by leaving interpretative space between those different representations, it asks the viewer to make their own connections — to find the still's spot on the video, to revisit and reassess Bedford Avenue and other urban labels. While Johae's own interests and remarks are distinctly articulated, the project — to its merit — extends beyond itself and takes the viewer on a journey through Brooklyn, by means of investigation and creative interpretation, leaving behind new questions about an unknown familiar territory.

For publication in this journal, *bedford avenue — brooklyn — ny* has been re-edited. A large number of stills, taken at regular intervals, recreate the spatio-temporal experience of the two videos and take the reader along Bedford Avenue while they move through the pages. Here, *bedford avenue — brooklyn — ny* presents another close look at Bedford Avenue in a singular medium that replaces the videos' temporal succession with the spatial succession in the journal — potentially rearranged according to the reader's disposition to flick back and forth.

Carola Ebert

Sheepshead Bay
Emmons Avenue
Shore Parkway
Voorhies Avenue
Avenue Z
Avenue Y
Avenue X
Avenue W
Avenue V
Gravesend Neck Road
Avenue U
Avenue T
Avenue S
Avenue R
Quentin Road
Avenue P
Kings Highway
Avenue O
Avenue N
Avenue M
Avenue L
Avenue K
Avenue J
Avenue I
Campus Road
Glenwood Road
Farragut Road
Foster Avenue
Stephens Court
Flatbush Avenue
Newkirk Avenue
Avenue D
Clarendon Road
Cortelyou Road
Beverly Road
Tilden Avenue
Albemarle Road
Snyder Avenue
Erasmus Street
Church Avenue
Martense Street
Linden Boulevard
Lenox Road
Clarkson Avenue
Parkside Avenue
Winthrop Street
Hawthorne Street
Fenimore Street
Rutland Road
Midwood Street
Maple Street
Lincoln Road
Lefferts Avenue
Sterling Street
Empire Boulevard
Sullivan Place
Montgomery Street
Crown Street
Carroll Street
President Street
Union Street
Eastern Parkway
Lincoln Place
Saint Johns Place
Sterling Place

Park Place
Prospect Place
Saint Marks Avenue
Bergen Street
Dean Street
Pacific Street
Atlantic Avenue
Brevoort Place
Fulton Street
Halsey Street
Hancock Street
Jefferson Avenue
Putnam Avenue
Madison Street
Monroe Street
Gates Avenue
Quincy Street
Lexington Avenue
Greene Avenue
Clifton Place
Lafayette Avenue
Kosciuszko Street
De Kalb Avenue
Willoughby Avenue
Myrtle Avenue
Park Avenue
Flushing Avenue
Wallabout Street
Lynch Street
Heyward Street
Rutledge Street
Penn Street
Hewes Street
Hooper Street
Williamsburg Street
Rodney Street
Ross Street
Wilson Street
Taylor Street
Clymer Street
Morton Street
Division Avenue
S. 9th Street
S. 8th Street
Broadway
S. 6th Street
S. 5th Street
S. 4th Street
S. 3rd Street
S. 2nd Street
S. 1st Street
Grand Street
N. 1st Street
Metropolitan Avenue
N. 3rd Street
N. 4th Street
N. 5th Street
N. 6th Street
N. 7th Street
N. 8th Street
N. 9th Street
N. 10th Street
N. 11th Street
N. 12th Street
Lorimer Street
Manhattan Avenue

BY DESIGN:
EDITING THE CITY

Scott Page and Brian Phillips

Urban design exists nebulously between the recognized realms of planning, architecture, and landscape architecture. Traditionally, it has operated from the position that cities are physical objects that can be designed as formal, spatial configurations. However, it has become difficult to view the design of the contemporary city in purely physical terms. The physical city has hybridized itself with the virtual, fusing real, local conditions to global flows of people, money, goods, and images. We argue that a crucial shift is required in how urban designers view their roles in shaping cities to bring new relevance to the discipline. This new relevance should be embedded in how we read, and more importantly edit, the city in the design process.

The Emergent City

Nearly every piece of the city, old and new, from downtown blocks to the sprawling horizontal boxes of the suburbs are wired together by a mesh of sidewalks, highways, rail lines, fiber runs, and cell phone towers. The pulse of the metropolis is animated by innumerable, simultaneous electronic connections that link local environments to an infinite number of other environments, creating an ambient urbanism. In a perpetual state of flux, its networked infrastructure expands and contracts in tandem with new and/or improved modes of circulating people, goods, and information along those networks. The new city is characterized by changing dynamics related to control, mobility, and context.

CONTROL— Cities have always been the primary seats of political, economic, and religious significance, making urban spaces key instruments for control. Pope Sixtus V in Rome and Baron Hausmann in Paris both undertook aggressive acts of regularization to reorganize their urban patterns to facilitate circulation: in Rome, to streamline religious pilgrimages; and in Paris, to more efficiently navigate the medieval fabric and to quell social uprisings.[1] Cities were built and transformed by decree in a top-down manner.

Through the 20th century, the liberalization of markets and the influence of the banking industry shifted the power center of urban development increasingly out of the hands of government and into those of private developers and homeowners. Centralized decision-making and coordination became difficult as multiple development teams across several political jurisdictions worked simultaneously. Despite the rules imposed by zoning codes and comprehensive plans — land values, tax revenues, and political machinations are often deciding factors for development projects and their regulatory variances. Private entities often sponsor urban design plans in concert with government agencies, non-profit organizations, neighborhood associations, educational institutions, businesses, and banks. Urban designers are now but one voice in a much larger group of city design operatives that cross spatial boundaries and localities.

MOBILITY— Arguably, no single dynamic characterizes the contemporary city, more than mobility. Extensive transportation and communications networks have resulted in an entire culture of nomadic populations who ride the distributed metropolis in cars, on airplanes, and through the Internet. The remarkable advantages of computing were amplified as digital communications — by way of fiber optic infrastructure, wireless service, and the Internet — began to achieve conditions of virtual proximity — real-time exchanges — and new collaborative models. The impact is as profound, albeit radically different, for those effectively disconnected from these opportunities.

Some theorists began to warn us of the impending end of real space — that our abilities to be virtually anywhere would eclipse our desire to be any place in particular. However, there is little evidence pointing to the total consumption of the physical by the virtual. Thus far, we inhabit a hybridized reality where the physical and virtual compete, complement, and splinter each other. New opportunities for urban design lie in this in-between realm.

CONTEXT—The rapid expansion of time-space as facilitated by our increased mobility is clearly warping and displacing our sense of local environment. Today, our contexts are highly customized and greatly expanded, rife with multiple scales and very difficult to reduce to static relationships. It is no longer possible to draw a geographic halo around an urban element and feel as though an accurate sense of context has been identified.

The reaction of many urban designers to this trend has been to rely on traditional notions of contextualism whereby physical adjacencies, vernacular precedents, and local histories are defining characteristics. In their efforts to control the physical form of a given context, many urban designers view contextualism in direct opposition to individualism.

But each of our social contexts are personalized, and our values related to form and aesthetics are certainly as unique and diverse. As expressed by Koolhaas, "contextualism actually precludes a series of more complex and precise choices that could bring the actual context into focus."[2] An expanded context, due to splintering urban control and enhanced mobility, inhibits a single vantage point from which to view the city and offers dramatic challenges for city design.

A Changed View for Designing the City

> . . . Edited space can be life.
> —Martha Stewart [3]

A constant flow of new production and interactions is actively annotating, shaping, and filtering the city. While some lament the seeming lack of design in the contemporary metropolis, we believe the city is absolutely being designed by new marquee buildings, art installations, advertising campaigns, televised events, development subsidies, trade agreements, online travel guides and innumerable other elements. We must acknowledge the city of multiple views — a city in which the urban designer's ability to control development, reduce movement to a crawl, or demarcate meaningful physical contexts is limited.

Our focus is on the changing relationships between people, information, and real places caused by shifts in the structure of power and context. As noted by Howard Rheingold, "New technologies always create opportunities for power shifts, and at each stage from writing to the Internet, more and more power decentralizes."[4] The power shifts represent, in many ways, a kind of self-organizing system. This system is not explicitly designed; tools are available to create new means of communicating, coordinating, and interacting that were not anticipated by the original designers of those tools. Stephen Johnson and many others refer to these self-organizing theories as emergence. Johnson states, "A city is a kind of pattern-amplifying machine: its neighborhoods are a way of measuring and expressing the repeated behavior of larger collectives...you don't need regulations and city planners deliberately creating these structures. All you need are thousands of individuals and a few simple rules of interaction."[5] These ideas allow us to visualize a structure of the networked city — which we find to be more trajectory than form.

As a potential way forward, we submit the notion of editing as a way of understanding this new urban territory at the intersection of physical and digital space. Originally, *edit* and *editor* stem from the term *edere* — to bring forth, produce. It implies the making of something new by manipulating or recombining existing material. Various forms of editing exist including collage, montage, and sampling — and it is not our point to distinguish between them, or favor any particular operation. We use editing in its most inclusive form, as a cultural process of filtering.

Designer as Editor

> It's all language because if I make my mix out of my own stuff than that's recombinant . . . but, if you do your style on my take, who owns the mix? Is it you, is it me, is it the beats that came from the other records?
> —DJ Spooky [6]

Many creative disciplines have embraced techniques related to editing to create unique expressions. The control in these operations lies not in the design, but in the editing process itself. Duchamp's ready-mades observed the value of ordinary objects taken out of context, and Robert Rauschenberg, among other artists, mixed subject matters and media (photography, text, paint) to communicate edited messages. Television shows on numerous cable stations now mine their archives and recombine old footage in new ways, producing new programs from existing fragments. Sampling has driven new music for the past two decades to the point that many popular songs are simply remixes and new combinations of old songs. Editing, whether it is referred to as sampling, collage, or any other variant, is now so pervasive that we have become "a nation of copiers."[7] This form of editing is not simply about getting people information in easily manageable sound bites; it is a means of cultural production in itself.

Rowe and Koetter's *Collage City* explicitly recognized editing as a design process. They argued for an approach to urbanism that used the city's fabric of layered, fragmentary history as a basis for design. They quote Levi-Strauss on the *bricoleur*, ". . . the rules of his game are always to make do with 'whatever is at hand.'"[8] Reliance on individual perceptions to construct a concept of the whole were also critical to the mid-century urban experiments of the Situationist International. The Situationists' maps and collages reflected their interest in how the unique worldview and subjectivities of each individual could provide a new way of editing the city.

In certain ways, even in circles of traditional practice, urban designers have always been editors. In the backlash to the urban renewal movement, more community-oriented and small-scale design proliferated, with urban designers playing a central role in navigating the multiple networks of funding streams, clients, policy objectives, community values, and information through mapping, which entails editing relevant information. But in the wake of increasing access to information and rapid metropolitan change, current urban design practice has largely retreated to the tenets believed to be at its historic foundation: master plans that delineate a fixed product and design style proliferate as a basis for practice. The focus on an end product over process denies possibilities for discovering new techniques, relationships and strategies.

What Are We Editing?

> Information management — subduing the complexity of a large-scale human settlement — is the latent purpose of the city.
> —Stephen Johnson [9]

The way the city is read is a key issue in uncovering ways one might intervene within the contemporary metropolis. Cities are an ongoing record of many players and forces operating through global, regional, and local spheres of influence, utilizing tools and techniques that are permanent, ephemeral, invisible and strategic. They are clearinghouses of meaning, constructed by multiple images, representations and information sources that play a critical role in how people form perceptions. Beauregard points out that "people decide how to respond on the basis of meanings, not on the basis of facts."[10] The need for cities to compete on this level has led to the fact that "most government agencies engaged in economic development spend more time marketing the locality than planning and implementing physical changes to it."[11]

The development of mediated forms of information — from newsprint to television — has created an information culture that has profoundly impacted the representation and use of cities. With this information culture, only a portion of what we know or experience in cities is through direct physical contact. It is the tremendous volume of intelligence, experience, and knowledge, combined with the ability to make this databank widely available that interests us. An information culture has always existed in some form, but the increasing number of, and variations in, tools with which to download and browse urban information brings unprecedented ways to interact and understand the city. With the volume of information and means to distribute it exponentially growing, editing has become a fundamental state of being. As stated by Frances Dyson, "The ever-expanding, continuously on-call individual becomes another kind of interface, for ever screening, filtering, ignoring, accepting, and repressing the plethora of inputs, information and demands for action that absorb his or her private space and individual time."[12] It is this reliance on broadcast media as a filter for our perceptions that led Alfred Birnbaum, in his essay on media and Japanese culture, to write that "the *real Japan*, the post-culture media state, only exists in the last edit."[13]

Everyone is contributing to a particular edition of the city at any given moment — a perpetual, collective process of editing, publishing and revising. As discussed by Nigel Thrift, the increasing degree to which software is "informationalizing the city" through web-pages, smart highways, and mobile devices: "Cities are quite literally, being written."[14] Where we choose to live, set up business, shop, and recreate are all based on readings of the city created through this mediated but reflective environment, and all of our social and economic transactions become part of the script. With these multiple agendas, conceiving of and planning for a single city-form is problematic.

Traditionally, urban design has considered a project site to be a defined area of real estate. Are there other types of sites from which to design cities? This is being recognized by some urban designers as they use language such as "strategically staged surfaces,"[15] "interpretive landscapes,"[16] and "interpretive frameworks"[17] to redefine the spaces within which we work.

Response

DECODING AND REPRESENTING URBAN INFORMATION— The role of urban designer as an editor of visual information has always been a key aspect of the profession, but has become more important with the volume of urban data now available and new visualization methods. Extracting characteristics that are relevant to a particular project or client is of great value. The robust market for Geographic Information Systems (GIS) consulting — where urban designers and planners help clients manipulate existing or build new databases, and present them in maps, graphs, or other formats to analyze and make sense of the data — illustrates. Creative and revealing interpretations of urban data have been

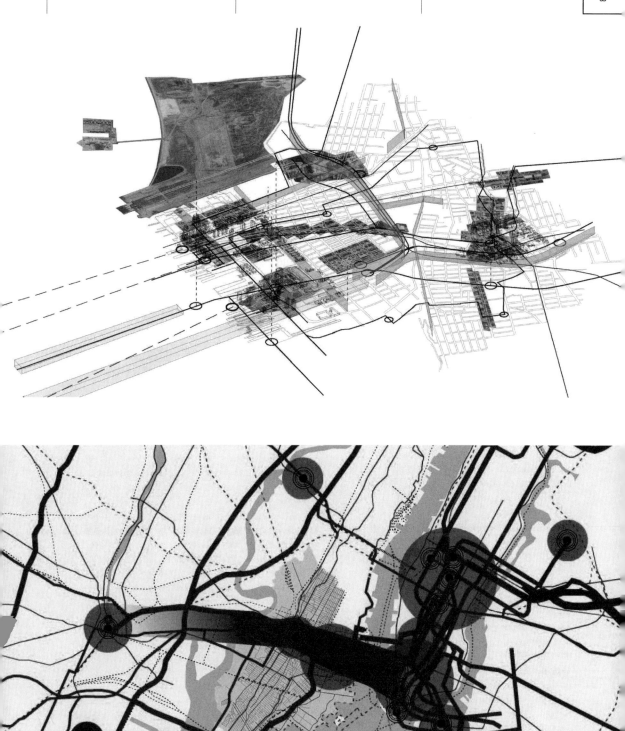

Jersey City intensity map

demonstrated through the dramatic computer images of Nadia Amoroso. Rafael Lozano-Hemmer has explored binding physical spaces with digital interfaces to enable more voices to visibly alter an environment. For these artists and others, the information of the city is not encoded in a static plan but designed to elicit different readings and perceptions of the city. They exist both within a computer interface and within the context of the city.

As part of a research project focused on Jersey City, NJ, we sought methods to map the physical and digital city simultaneously. By juxtaposing traditional and non-traditional urban information at different scales, we produced a series of images that presents an edited version of the dynamics shaping the city. Included here is an infrastructure map describing flow intensity for the region and an image of downtown which shows circulation infrastructure, barriers, and key destination enclaves. In Newark, NJ, we sought to re-present the city to itself, utilizing the air rights of an industrial district facing the NJ Turnpike. Activated by passing cars, the proposed video billboards stream real-time information and images in an effort to reinvent Newark's image in the minds of tens of thousands of commuters each day.

SHARED RESOURCES FOR INDIVIDUAL EDITING— A primary concern for the health of civic discourse in cities are the disparate opportunities new digital infrastructures offer different populations. Manuel Castells characterizes this as the rise of a "dual" city that is "socially and spatially polarized."[18] All cities in the United States contain neighborhoods that have become profoundly disconnected, effectively cut off from economic opportunities, jobs, and infrastructure. Battling tremendous levels of poverty, crime, and physical decay, proposed solutions for these environments are often based in building new physical fabric. Other potential opportunities lie in merging the bottom-up planning and organizing that already occurs in many impoverished neighborhoods with the capabilities of urban software: shared tools that enable people to individually edit their relationship to an expanding world based on their own interests. Neighborhood tool boxes can combine traditional services with new technologies, enabling local residents to positively act on their environments without the need for urban designers or planners to determine an outcome. The design challenge is to create programs that facilitate enhanced communication and set up only a few rules of interaction. As Howard Rheingold said, "the knowledge and technologies that triggered the jump from clan to tribe to nation to market to network all shared one characteristic: they each amplified the

way individual humans think and communicate, and magnified their ability to share what they know."[19]

This strategy was explored in a plan completed for Hudson County, NJ that binds new technologies to physical improvements. It did not seek a comprehensive end product. Rather we proposed a series of distributed shared resources for digital initiatives and networked services tied to focused, place-specific investment. An example of such a place-specific facility is best illustrated by the proposed EastgateLIVE! Arts Center in Washington DC. It has been conceived as a facility to combine skill-building and performance in a way that brings profitable, creative production to a challenged urban community. The program includes art, fashion and sound studios where a major record label would share its expertise through education and training programs. A key urban component of the project is the intent to provide a bridge between neighborhood and city through digital linkages and networked programs.

PHYSICAL PLACES EDITING DIGITAL INFORMATION— Browsable banks of data have become a standard way to filter urban places. Until recently, travel guides, films, and face-to-face accounts were the only ways to connect with other places in lieu of having actually been there. Today, the Internet provides numerous methods to sort through urban information in highly customized ways. We now see an increased integration and awareness of urban software that until recently was relegated to the back doors of city-space.

As tools like mobile phones become "remote controls for the physical world,"[20] we emphasize the need for urban designers to consider these developments in their projects and research. As these devices move further into the civic realm and merge with location awareness technology, our physical cities can, and will, provide a key methodology for editing digital information. Digital *Post-it* notes accessible by cell phones within physical proximity to a specific place and on line games like Bot-Fighters — that integrate the city into the actual playing of the game — are a few recent examples. As Dennis Frenchman states, "Our experience of the environment — and in turn its legibility — is shaped by what we know about it and what we can learn from it."[21] Recognizing that much urban software is developed in research institutions, urban designers have little impact on the specific technologies themselves. How they are applied to city space, however, is rife with possibilities.

Spaces that offer a co-presence of digital information and physical assets will benefit far more than one-dimensional approaches that privilege one kind of experience explicitly over another. This has

Global
Regional
Local

Tools

Theater
Lighting/Sound
Writing
Production
Live Drama
Live Dance

Performing Arts

Design
Marketing
Textiles

Fashion Design

Music Recording
Engineering
Production
Marketing
Instrument/Voice Training
Internships

Music

Painting
Photography
Graphic Design
Web Design
Animation
Cartooning
Fundamental Drawings

Visual Arts

Basic Computer Skills
GED Prep / Testing
Job Readiness
Budget/Credit Counseling
Homeownership Prep
Parenting Counseling
Athletic Tutoring

Life Skills

Music Store
Cafe
Books
Ticket Sales
Entrepreneurship Training
Library
Shared Facilities

Economic Development

Production

→ *Dramatic Productions*
→ *Dance Productions*
→ *Children's Theater*
→ *Film Screening*
→ *Fashion Shows*
→ *Garment Sales*
→ *Holiday Concerts*
→ *Music Sales*
→ *Music Performance*
→ *Merchandise*
→ *Web Design Consulting*
→ *Art Exhibitions*
→ *Craft Shows*
→ *Education*
→ *Literacy Programs*
→ *Housing Investment*
→ *Job Creation*
→ *Small Business Assistance*
→ *Business Incubators*

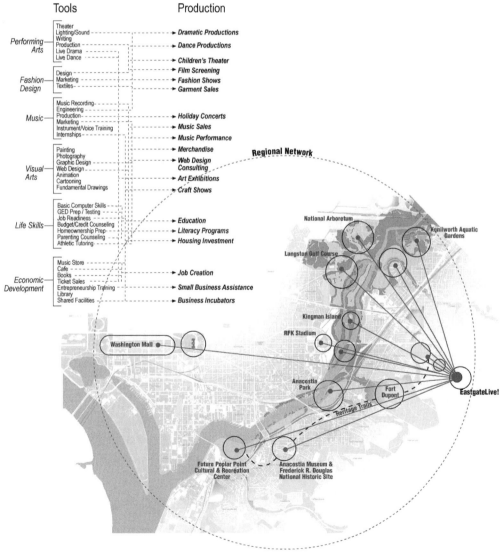

Regional Network

National Arboretum

Kenilworth Aquatic Gardens

Langston Golf Course

Kingman Island

RFK Stadium

Washington Mall

Anacostia Park

Fort Dupont

Heritage Trails

EastgateLive!

Future Poplar Point Cultural & Recreation Center

Anacostia Museum & Frederick R. Douglas National Historic Site

EastgateLIVE! skill-building and performance map

driven our project to revitalize the distressed APM community in North Philadelphia. The project seeks to create a new interface between Temple University and the neighborhood, inhabiting a stretch of vacant land that isolates both. Our objective was to seek new ways of instilling communication between different sets of people, empowering residents and enabling them to understand their community by integrating digital information into physical space. Focused around a rail corridor and station, a networked series of interfaces were proposed in key public spaces. Updated in real-time, the interfaces and Web site will provide a browsable and concentrated resource of local information. The technology initiatives are intended to expand with the participation of local users in concert with a focused physical plan designed to reinforce local connections.

Summary

While design culture in general has nearly reached a fever pitch of creative expression, urban design remains quietly entrenched in formal operations. We believe urban design should be an interpretive process where editing plays a key role in conceptually bridging the digital and physical worlds. The contemporary urban condition presents opportunities for design in the purest sense — moments of interpretation, empowerment, play, and deviance. It is instructive to consider what Simon Sadler identifies as a golden age of collaborative, creative energy that inspired the Situationist International. He describes it as, "a time when artists, architects, and designers had pursued disparate, open-ended experiments; a time when the conditions of modern life — above all, the relationship between man and machine — had been addressed head-on."[22] If urbanism occurs between the spheres of information and physical place, our work must become dynamic, operating to some degree in both worlds.

Scott Page is an Associate and urban designer with Wallace Roberts & Todd, LLC, a planning, urban design, architecture and landscape architecture firm based in Philadelphia. Scott is a lecturer at the University of Pennsylvania's School of Design in the Department of City and Regional Planning. He holds degrees from Georgia Tech and the University of Pennsylvania.

Brian Phillips is an architect, urban designer and an Associate with Wallace Roberts & Todd, LLC. He is an adjunct faculty member at the Drexel University College of Media Arts and Design in Philadelphia, where he teaches architecture and urbanism. He holds degrees from the University of Oklahoma and the University of Pennsylvania.

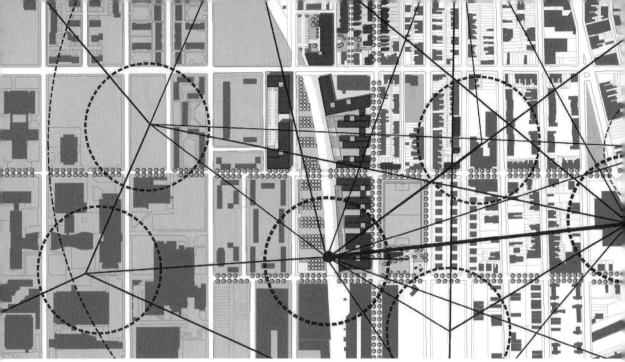

APM interfaces

NOTES

1. Frampton, Kenneth. *Modern Architecture: A Critical History*. London: Thames and Hudson, 1980. Pg. 24.
2. Koolhaas, Rem and Bruce Mau. *S,M,L,XL*. New York: Monacelli Press, 1995.
3. Colomina, Beatriz. "Martha Stewart is Editing Your Life." *Wired*. Jun 2003.
4. Rheingold, Howard. *Smart Mobs: The Next Social Revolution*. Cambridge: Perseus Publishing, 2003.
5. Johnson, Stephen. *Emergence: The Connected Lives of Ants, Brains, Cities, and Software*. New York: Touchstone, 2001.
6. DJ Spooky. "Conversation." *Riddim Warfare*. September 21, 1998. Outpost Records.
7. Leland, John. "Beyond File-Sharing, a Nation of Copiers." *New York Times*, September 14, 2003. Section 9, Page 1, Column 2.
8. Rowe, Colin and Fred Koetter. *Collage City*. Boston: Birkhauser, 1980.
9. Ibid, Johnson.
10. Ploger, John. "Millenium Urbanism — Discursive Planning." *European Urban and Regional Studies*. 8.1 (2001).

11. Holcomb, Briavel. "Place Marketing: Using Media to Promote Cities." *Imaging the City*. Eds. Lawrence J. Vale and Sam Brass Warner Jr. New Brunswick: Center for Urban Policy Research, 2001.
12. Dyson, Frances. "'Space,' 'Being,' and Other Fictions in the Domain of the Virtual." *The Virtual Dimension: Architecture, Representation, and Crash Culture*. Ed. John Beckmann. New York: Princeton Architectural Press, 1998.
13. Birnbaum, Alfred. "Eizoticism." *Sites: Architecture 24*. Eds. Ronald Christ and Dennis Dolens. Lumen Press, 1992.
14. Thrift, Nigel. "Software Writing Cities." *Address to Information and the Urban Future Conference at NYU (February 2001)*. <http://www.informationcity.org/events/feb26/thrift-presentation/Thrift.pdf>
15. Wall, Alex. "Programming the Urban Surface." *Recovering Landscape: Essays in Contemporary Landscape Architecture*. Ed. James Corner. New York: Princeton Architectural Press, 1999.
16. Frenchman, Dennis. "Narrative Places and the New Practice of Urban Design." *Imaging the City*. Eds. Lawrence J. Vale and Sam Brass Warner, Jr. New Brunswick: Center for Urban Policy Research, 2001.
17. Vale, Lawrence J. "New Public Realms: Re-imaging the City-Region." *Imaging the City*. Ed. Lawrence J. Vale and Sam Bass Warner, Jr. New Brunswick: Center for Urban Policy Research, 2001.
18. Castells, Manuel. "The Informational City is a Dual City: Can it be Reversed?" *High Technology and Low Income Communities: Prospects for the Positive Use of Advanced Information Technology*. Eds. Donald A. Schon, Bish Sanyal and William J. Mitchell. Cambridge: MIT Press, 1999.
19. Ibid, Rheingold.
20. Ibid, Rheingold.
21. Ibid, Frenchman.
22. Sadler, Simon. The Situationist City. Cambridge: MIT Press, 1999.

BAYTOWN MUSEUM OF NETWORK ARCHEOLOGY

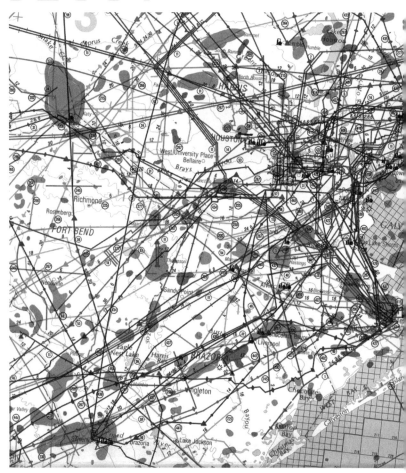

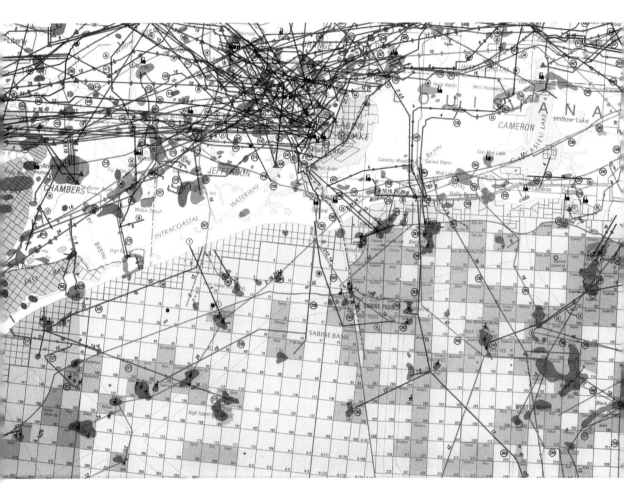

Paul Schuette

At the inception of the space race, John Kennedy declared space to be the "new ocean," a realm of infinite exploration, open for yet another wave of the modernist project. If the origins of the modern project rested in the aspirations for humans to know all that was within their grasp, this new challenge presented an unusual paradox. The quest was large enough to blow apart the idea of a contained body of knowledge, a graspable finite canon. The very idea of the secular quest for knowledge became so large that it has taken on a role of a sort of deity.

But while these ideas of infinite exploration may seem especially appropriate for the cosmos, they also have a relevance to earthbound constructions, the artifacts and detritus of humanity. It is here that the modernist project of the museum becomes important. The museum is central to the modern project, a project of continual collecting, sorting, and classification. However, what if the charge of the museum is the collection of infrastructure? How can infrastructure, which typically stretches beyond *thing-ness*, beyond collection, be classified, sorted and understood? Does it lie beyond the reach of the museum as a modern project, or does it continue to push the boundaries of the museum? These are some of the questions that the Baytown Museum of Network Archaeology poses.

The Baytown Museum of Network Archaeology, or BMNA, is both a physical construction and a body of information which serves to excavate that construction. The museum's goal is to reveal physical infrastructures that allow the city of Baytown, Texas to function as a huge oil-based economic generator. Its primary goal is one of illuminating both the mechanisms of production and how they ultimately lead to the consumption of goods that a first-world consumer may encounter hundreds of times per day. The BMNA uses the city of Baytown as a sort of measuring device. Like a strange parasite, the museum attaches to the infrastructure of the city itself — sometimes hidden and sometimes not — in order to trace the flow of petrochemical goods and products into, within and out of Baytown.

The city of Baytown, Texas, approximately 30 miles east of Houston, can be described as one of the primary generators of Houston's post-World War II rise from city to megalopolis. The city sits adjacent to the Houston Ship Channel, which has spawned the international port of call, the Port of Houston. Within its borders, Baytown witnessed the rise and proliferation of what might be called the 20th century's super-commodity, oil. In the early twentieth century, oil producers extracted millions of barrels of crude oil within Baytown and processed them within the city's many refineries. As demands for synthetic products grew during World War II, Baytown's refineries and oil processing facilities produced plastics that would be used for many synthetic products. Baytown contains the largest refinery in the United States, and the second largest in the world.

The structure of the BMNA is a multi-tiered system moving from the general to the specific. The top tier of the BMNA is the network. The network encompasses all petrochemical infrastructures that move in, within, and out of Baytown. Although the BMNA is centered within the city of Baytown itself, its central subject, petrochemical infrastructure, continues endlessly into the world. The network tier of the BMNA consists of three divisions: absorption, processing and release. Each of these respective divisions of the museum corresponds to the flow direction of petrochemical substances into, within, or out of Baytown.

The second tier of the BMNA is the sub-network. The sub-network is a path within the network itself, which typically describes a piece of infrastructure or consumption of petrochemical goods. Each sub-network functions as a narrative. As a museum patron moves through a sub-network, changes at each node indicate the progression in the narrative of that sub-network.

Each sub-network has a ten-watt AM radio station associated with it. As patrons of the museum move through the BMNA, they may listen to narratives, which further describe the logic of each sub-network. The sub-network tier functions as the museum exhibition space. Although there are only five sub-networks in the current conception of the BMNA, many more could be added to one of the larger network tiers, absorption, processing, and release. Each sub-network expands upon the myth of petrochemical production and consumption.

In this essay, I will focus on the node, a space that visitors of the BMNA initially encounter in their exploration of the museum. Although the smallest element in the BMNA, the node relates the patron to larger relationships within the BMNA as a whole.

Model in performance: podiums play relevant sound clips and trigger lighted node locations

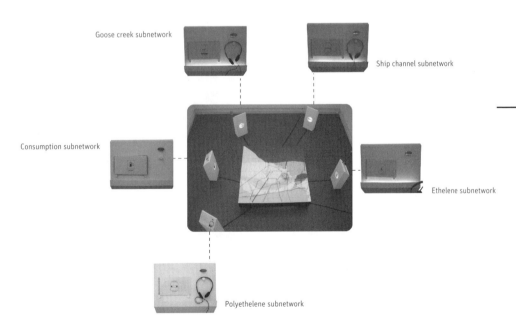

Goose creek subnetwork

Ship channel subnetwork

Consumption subnetwork

Ethelene subnetwork

Polyethelene subnetwork

Museum model: each podium presents information about sub-networks

Ship channel sub-network node

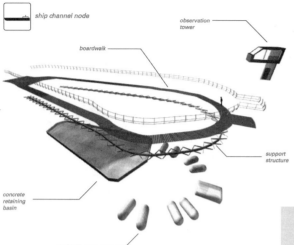

ship channel node

observation
tower

boardwalk

support
structure

concrete
retaining
basin

pontoons

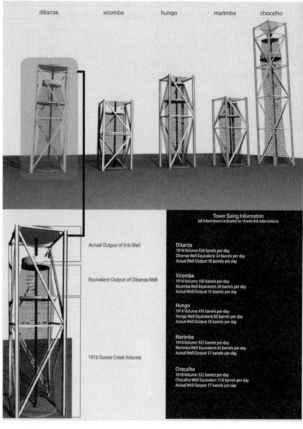

dikanza   xicomba   hungo   marimba   chocalho

Actual Output of this Well

Equivalent Output of Dikanza Well

1916 Goose Creek Volume

Tower Sizing Information
(all information is indicated on 10 watt AM radio stations)

Dikanza
1916 Volume: 526 barrels per day
Dikanza Well Equivalent: 54 barrels per day
Actual Well Output: 16 barrels per day

Xicomba
1916 Volume: 192 barrels per day
Xicomba Well Equivalent: 28 barrels per day
Actual Well Output: 15 barrels per day

Hungo
1916 Volume: 476 barrels per day
Hungo Well Equivalent: 60 barrels per day
Actual Well Output: 15 barrels per day

Marimba
1916 Volume: 322 barrels per day
Marimba Well Equivalent: 45 barrels per day
Actual Well Output: 17 barrels per day

Chocalho
1916 Volume: 322 barrels per day
Chocalho Well Equivalent: 116 barrels per day
Actual Well Output: 17 barrels per day

Goose Creek sub-netowrk node

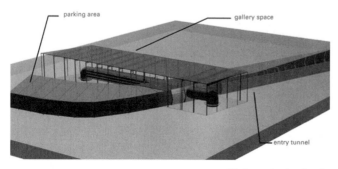

parking area   gallery space

entry tunnel

Ethylene sub-network node

Initial Approach — Deliberate Entry, Chance Encounter

There are two ways of encountering and entering the BMNA. In the *deliberate entry* approach, the BMNA is a destination. Thousands of young schoolchildren from the greater metropolitan Houston region, college students from the Midwest, and tourists visiting Houston are all potential user groups who might come to Baytown in search of the BMNA.

Two entry nodes serve this audience, both located along Interstate 10 which bisects the current BMNA. Entry nodes are information distribution points for museum visitors. They show a map of the existing BMNA and indicate where the absorption, processing, and release infrastructures of the BMNA lie within the city of Baytown. They also indicate where the existing sub-networks plug into the BMNA, thus indicating locations of all museum nodes within the city of Baytown. Thus the entry nodes provide for a clear understanding of how to take a complete tour of the BMNA.

Since the BMNA is a continually expanding project, its form of representation must be flexible. In her book *On Longing*, Susan Stewart states that "the writing of miniaturization does not want to call attention to itself or to its author; rather, it continually refers to the physical world."[1] Initial miniaturizations of the museum might be easy to contain, and could easily take the form of Civil War battlefield maps, indicating areas of activity.

However, as the museum expands out from Baytown and attaches itself to other petrochemical systems, its miniaturized form would expand greatly, calling more attention to the entry nodes themselves than to the museum. This problem would be easily solved through digital miniaturization, interactive maps and guides on the Internet. These nodes would only contain information concerning specific regions of the museum.

The second way of approaching and entering the BMNA is through a chance encounter with one of the nodes in the system. This mode of encounter is how a majority of the users, whether intentionally or not, move through the BMNA. Thousands of people live within the city of Baytown, and thousands more pass through its boundaries every day. Because of this, it is probable that an individual may encounter a node, an audio clip, signage — or all of the above — that relate to the BMNA. Most sub-networks are arranged in a linear fashion, so one moves through them in a narrative manner. However, if the majority of museum users are unintentional users, what does this imply for the physical form of the BMNA, with its large linear components?

Hopefully, curiosity would drive an individual to seek to understand the larger pieces of the museum. Certain elements of the BMNA are as banal as road signage, and thus not as likely to incite an individual to explore the system further. However, other items are large anomalies within Baytown's landscape. For example at the end of the BMNA polyethylene sub-network, a seventy-foot high tower sits at the side of the road. Seeking to understand this anomaly as it relates to others could prompt an individual to move further through the BMNA.

The discrete nature of the nodes, and the possibility of random encounters with them, highlight Deleuze's concept of the virtual in the BMNA. As Deleuze describes it, the virtual is the possible, a possibility that seeks realization. Like memory, which cannot be ascribed to any one location and yet implies a network of related thoughts and images, the virtual implies every element of the entirety of a network.[2] Thus, encoded in one node is the information of a larger system of sub-networks; encoded within that is the larger shape of the network itself. Each piece of the BMNA: the AM radio broadcasts, the signage, and the nodes themselves, refer to something much larger than themselves. While each discrete element of the museum might have a significant role to play in and of itself — the dissemination of a specific piece of information, or the staging of a certain view — each also refers to a much larger picture of the overall network. Not only does each existing element of the museum refer to all other existing elements of the BMNA, but it also suggests all potential interventions that might take place within the museum. Thus, nodes that do not yet exist — and sub-networks that are not yet in place — are referred to through the existence of nodes and sub-networks, and the infrastructure that they seek to reveal. The potential of the entire network can be referred to through each discrete element in the system.

The Node and Beyond

In his book on urban design, *The Image of the City*, Kevin Lynch describes nodes as "strategic foci into which the observer can enter typically either junctions of paths, or concentrations of some characteristic."[3] Although the nodes of the BMNA work in a very different context than the dense urban conditions that Lynch describes in his book, they function in a similar way. Each node provides a space where a museum user can enter and further understand a narrative behind a specific piece of petrochemical infrastructure. Signage and AM radio broadcasts provide certain information to the museum patron, but the charge of the node is to make that information have physicality. The three modes of information distribution within the BMNA, the signage, the AM radio broadcast, and the physical module are integral to the working of one node. The fact that there are three modes of information dissemination also increases the possibilities of interaction between the casual driver through and the BMNA as he or she moves through Baytown.

The modular architecture of the node provides a simple structure, which allows all of the upper tiers of the museum to function together. Michel de Certeau's descriptions of the literary device synecdoche provide a reference to this idea of the structure of a system. Synecdoche is a device in which a part represents a much larger whole. De Certeau describes synecdoche as enlarging "a spatial element in order to make it play the role of a *more*."[4] In certain nodes, this enlarging happens quite literally. At the nodes of the ethylene sub-network, a large pipe seems to emerge from the ground. This pipe rests directly over where the actual ethylene pipeline runs underground and provides the structure for the display of the node's artifacts. The use of synecdoche is not quite as extreme in other sub-networks. However, the fact that each module works as a symbol for the sub-network demonstrates the use of synecdoche in the museum on some level. Through its modular nature, each node plays the role of an agent representing the entire sub-network.

The relationship between the nodes varies throughout the museum. Certain nodes are up to two miles apart from one another. Although these distances are easily traversed by automobile, the primary means of moving through the museum, each node may lie in a very different context. For example, in one sub-network, one node might rest at the edge of a refinery, while another may be within a housing subdivision. Different local user groups may potentially appropriate nodes for wide-ranging activities. The nodes' simple architecture allows each node to continue to read as part of a larger sub-network unless it is radically altered. However, slight alterations and appropriations have the possibility of creating interesting and unexpected relationships between the museum and the city of Baytown.

While unexpected changes occurring with the components of the museum may create new relationships between the city and the museum, changes in the larger global economic conditions may create a new role for the BMNA as a whole. The main thrust of the BMNA is to reveal how Baytown is a huge petrochemical-based economic generator for the greater Houston area. However, as a most extreme case, what if the petrochemical industry shifted in the coming century? What if automobiles began to rely less on gasoline and turned again to alternative fuel sources? Not only would this have huge ramifications for the city of Baytown and the people who work in its many refineries but also for the BMNA as well.

I use the term *archaeology* within the title of the BMNA to refer to an idea of artifacts, objects that point to the existence of a much larger social condition. In the case of BMNA, the artifacts point to a society that is inextricably tied to the production and consumption of petrochemical products. The term archaeology would have a very different meaning in relation to the BMNA if elements of the petrochemical industry ceased to exist. Entire sub-networks would become artifacts in a different sense, pointing to rituals of consumption and use of a past society. Eventually if petrochemical production ceased altogether — which someday due to limited raw materials it will be forced to do — the museum itself might become a giant artifact.

This extreme situation points to a much more immediate issue in the conception of the BMNA, scale. While scale has been an implicit player throughout this discussion, its relationship to the BMNA and the world must be addressed. Although the BMNA currently resides solely within the limits of Baytown, it has the potential to spread out into the world tracing the movements of petrochemicals and their ubiquitous consumption. It is here that the museum could begin to overwhelm the system it is revealing. Just as Borges tells of an empire that attempted to make a full-scale map of itself, thus doubling it own existence, so the BMNA might create an empire out of itself.

Rather than create a curated empire, the BMNA might be able to challenge contemporary conceptions of the museum through a very different strategy. This strategy would mandate that the BMNA reside within the boundaries of Baytown. While expansion is necessary for the museum's continued mission, all expansion would take place within the city. Just as petrochemical infrastructure extends out of Baytown and into the world, the sub-networks of the museum would point to those outside infrastructures without extending to them — the Goose Creek Extraction sub-network already does this. However, just as the disjunctions that exist between the AM radio perspective and the curatorial perspective promote an active and critical participation from the museum user, so could the containment of the museum. It encourages museum users to follow infrastructure into the world and to increase their awareness of petrochemical production. This production results in hundreds of commodities they might see and sometimes consume on a daily basis. In promoting this awareness, the BMNA leaves open the possibilities that other museums and methods of revealing might appear throughout the world through the agency of former BMNA users.

In this scenario the BMNA continues a tradition of the modern project while simultaneously pushing the boundaries — both in a literal and figurative sense — for the notion of a museum. Perhaps one of the greatest disjunctions between the modern project and the conception of a museum is the mediation of the curator. The secular subject is empowered as an authority to mediate a canon of knowledge and the artifacts that represent it. While initially an authority is needed to establish the BMNA, its continued existence demands the intervention of designers, curators, and other individuals to expand it within Baytown. At this point, the BMNA becomes a loose organization of myths and narratives surrounding petrochemicals. As users of the BMNA create other local museums like the BMNA elsewhere, the museum becomes even looser while the subject applies its principles. In a full realization of a modern project, the world becomes the museum and we become its curators.

Paul Schuette has a BA in Architecture from Columbia University and received a Master of Architecture from the Rice University in 2003. While at Rice, he received the Pittman Award to study overlaps in infrastructural development in pre-colonial and contemporary Peru. He currently lives and works in Paris, France.

Oil and natural gas pipelines between Houston and Beaumont, TX

NOTES

1. Susan Stewart, *On Longing: Narratives of the Miniature, the Gigantic, the Souvenir and the Collection.* Baltimore: Johns Hopkins University Press, 1984.
2. Gilles Deleuze, *Difference and Repetition.* New York: the Athlone Press Limited, 1994.
3. Kevin Lynch, *The Image of the City.* Cambridge: MIT Press, 1960.
4. Michel DeCerteau, *The Practice of Everyday Life.* Berkeley: University of California Press, 1984.

At Least 6 Said Killed in Bombing in Iraq

Okay

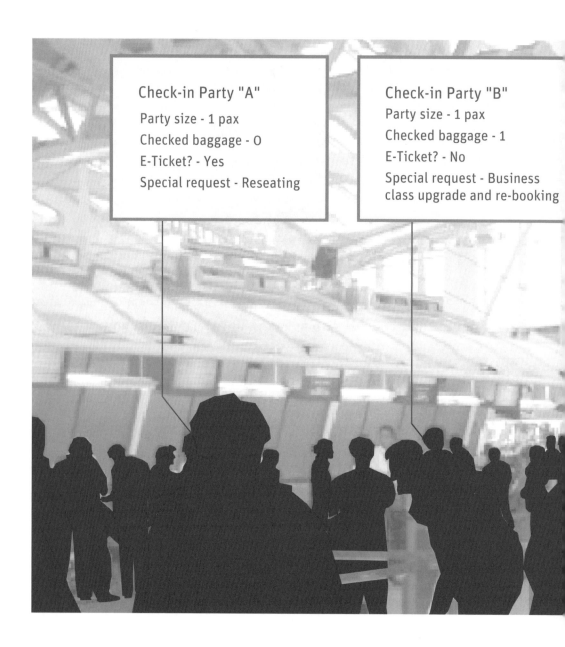

Check-in Party "A"

Party size - 1 pax
Checked baggage - 0
E-Ticket? - Yes
Special request - Reseating

Check-in Party "B"

Party size - 1 pax
Checked baggage - 1
E-Ticket? - No
Special request - Business class upgrade and re-booking

NEXTERM

EMERGING DIRECTIONS IN RECONCEPTUALIZING
THE AIRPORT PASSENGER TERMINAL

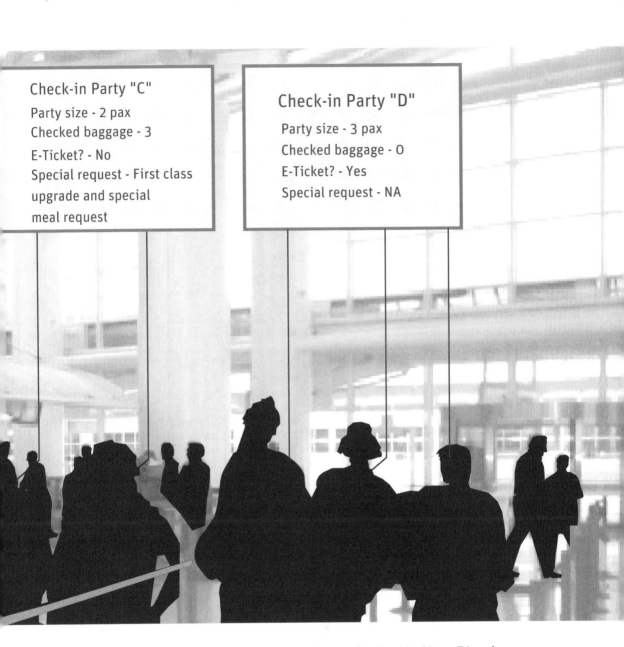

Check-in Party "C"

Party size - 2 pax
Checked baggage - 3
E-Ticket? - No
Special request - First class
upgrade and special
meal request

Check-in Party "D"

Party size - 3 pax
Checked baggage - 0
E-Ticket? - Yes
Special request - NA

Derrick K.Y. Choi

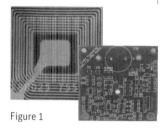

Figure 1

Introduction

The field of airport terminal planning and design, probably more than any other discipline, has been radically transformed on programmatic and spatial terms in direct response to the events of September 11, 2001, and ensuing global economic impacts. One of the most noticeable consequences of the various drivers transforming the passenger terminal typology is the automation and proliferation of virtual and multi-media processes in the airport passenger travel experience.

Airport passenger terminal operations and physical space utilization have become increasingly negotiated through alternative technology applications — such as Internet-based and wireless-based media, radio-frequency identification (RFID) applications, mobile telecommunications, Smart Cards, biometrics, and integrated information technology infrastructures. As such, emerging conditions — physical and otherwise — methods of data exchange, passenger flows, and communications have begun to yield distinct, new spatial and operational infrastructures. These conditions have re-conceptualized extant processes, formal conditions, and civic relationships facilitated by transportation infrastructure as we know of it. These emerging relationships are largely the consequences of recent automation of the passenger experience in transportation. Not dissimilar from the automation of the banking industry, *self-service* is rapidly becoming a ubiquitous component of the air travel experience. This paradigm shift in passenger check-in technology and processing suggests a potential to radically re-think the contemporary airport experience — spatially, operationally, and culturally.

Established conventions of transportation such as the passenger ticketing and check-in process, epitomized by grand ticketing halls including the original John F. Kennedy International Air Terminal or Grand Central Station in New York are rapidly becoming vestiges of the past, particularly in the industry context of airline operational cost containment and the emergence of, automated systems. Nevertheless, the effects of airport terminal conventions make an impact on the way travelers negotiate through these facilities. In that light, the traveling public has gradually adopted the idea of self check-in and electronic ticketing. As airlines continue to reorganize their finances and re-prioritize their physical and infrastructural development objectives, conventional terminology, including in-flight meals, checking-in, and ticketing, will take on new meaning.

Background — The Post 9/11 Airport

Since the events of September 11, 2001, the aviation industry has been radically altered, unlike any other period in its century-old evolution. Virtually unconstrained airport growth and associated infrastructural development came to an abrupt halt due in large part to the cumulative effects of domestic recession and major security concerns. Airline, airport, and federal regulatory constraints following September 11 yielded a desperate environment of survival largely characterized by historically low travel demand, airline cost-retrenchment, overall airport revenue reduction, and limited federal security staffing.

Technology applications and process automation, more than other proverbial quick-fixes, have been identified, even prior to September 11, as a key resource in mitigating passenger inconvenience and restoring confidence in airports, overall profitability to airlines, and a competitive edge for airport operators. As such, in this economic climate, technology applications and new operational processes have emerged as the preferred alternatives to costly physical expansion and airline staffing increases.

New Realities and Ensuing Challenges

The evolution of the airport passenger terminal typology formally and programmatically is by and large more a function of economics than any other drivers. Technology applications reflective of this trend include the recent introduction and deployment of two self-serve tools: passenger self check-in kiosks and Internet-based check-in systems. Both have decentralized the check-in paradigm within the boundaries of the traditional, dedicated spatial program. Many current passenger functions, including ticketing and duty-free shopping, can now be totally removed from the airport boundary devoid of any airport or airline intervention — in the convenience of private

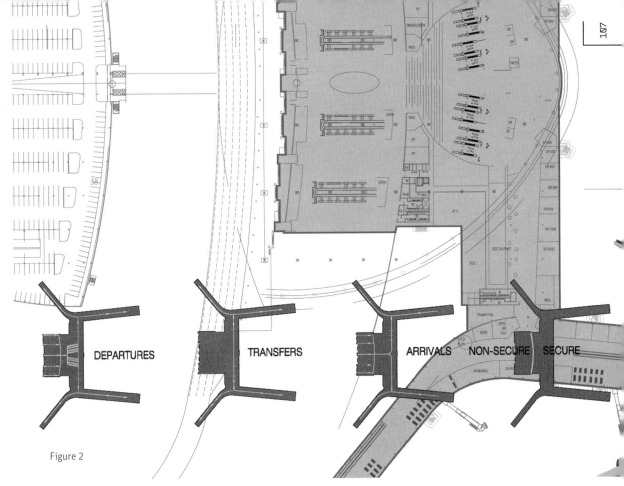

DEPARTURES   TRANSFERS   ARRIVALS   NON-SECURE   SECURE

Figure 2

Internet access or remote facilities. Currently being tested in combination with existing check-in processes, Smart Card technology embeds passenger passport and traveler information in a cell phone chip, and utilizes biometric authentication to validate the identity of the chip holder. In Hong Kong, passports for international travel can be swiped through select airline ticketing kiosks to further reduce the need for staff. Current manufacturing and distribution technology, such as radio-frequency identification (RFID), may have a profound effect on airport operations, especially in passenger processing and baggage handling and tracking. RFID, however, has been slow to break into the airport market due to its relatively high operational cost, at approximately five cents per RFID tag (Figure 1).

The recently hardened federal firewall of (in)security for passenger terminals and around airport perimeters, may have temporarily discouraged the notion of airport space as an alternative public arena, but it has also unwittingly incubated the growth and proliferation of new social networks and market opportunities that transcend the spatial and material limitations of the passenger terminal building itself. The recent spending increase at airport concession facilities and the proliferation of wireless access throughout domestic airports are indicative of these new modes of inhabitation. In recent years, the emergence of cell-phone parking lots adjacent to passenger terminals, where drivers temporarily park while awaiting the call from an arriving passenger, illustrates the emergence of vastly new ways of meeting and greeting the arriving passenger at the airport by taking full advantage of the proliferation and convenience of personal cellular telecommunications.

Decades-old planning conventions and standard design and planning guidelines for passenger terminal buildings are being further exacerbated by new security requirements and rising passenger usage trends toward earlier arrivals and worsening congestion in terminals. Buildings produced in the new reality of airport passenger terminal design and planning are faced with questions of how they will stand up to the new industry performance requirements and operational expectations. While passenger terminal buildings will continue — perhaps for some time — to serve basic operational functions, including the enplaning, deplaning, and connecting of passengers and baggage (Figure 2), they will continue to evolve and transform as dictated by market forces in the commercial aviation industry.

The passenger terminal building continues to evolve and respond to myriad factors, including:

DEMOGRAPHICS— Historically, air travel has been one of the few efficient sources of transcontinental mobility in the United States. As such, the proliferation and affordability of air travel has led to its democratization. Especially due to the dramatic growth of the low-fare airline industry, traveler demographics have diversified significantly over the last decade, especially among the retired or elderly, students, and families, each with unique air travel expectations (Figure 4). This is a significant departure from the early post-war era when air travel was a luxury few could afford. Today, some of the handful of profitable domestic U.S. airlines are low-fare carriers that are devoid of high overhead, operational costs, and labor union complications. As we look to the next century of air transportation, the passenger terminal, like shopping malls and other major public commercial facilities, must be even more responsive to the ever-changing and ever-diversifying needs of its users.

MARKETS— As commercial aviation market demand, operating standards, and regulatory framework change, so must the physical facilities that serve the industry. In this competitive, deregulated landscape, airports have further defined themselves in accordance to the distinct markets that they serve. Unique characteristics and airline performance expectations have been gradually defined for business travel, discretionary or *leisure* travel, distinct regional destinations, and as hub and origin-and-destination markets. As such, passenger terminal solutions have emerged as uniquely distinct; for myriad reasons, as no one airport is quite like the other.

REGULATORY FACTORS— Since the inception of the Aviation and Transportation Security Act of 2001 (ATSA), sweeping changes including the federalization of airport checkpoints and the screening of checked passenger baggage have put significant pressure on terminal availability, as well as resources to staff screening facilities. As the physical and staff capacity in most passenger terminals are being pushed to their limits, technology and optimization solutions are critical to helping airports do more with less. In this light, technology must also make the federal screening process as unobtrusive, or invisible, as possible.

AIRLINE OPERATIONAL AND FINANCIAL PRIORITIES— As airlines cope with recovering passenger demand and increasing costs, the deployment of new technologies and passenger processing approaches have been accelerated to ensure that the operating costs are in line with overall revenue. This process of cost optimization will have a significant implication on the overall staff and physical facility needs for future airport operations.

The NexTerm Initiative

The aforementioned near-term challenges are strategic opportunities to redefine the passenger terminal typology to address these new realities

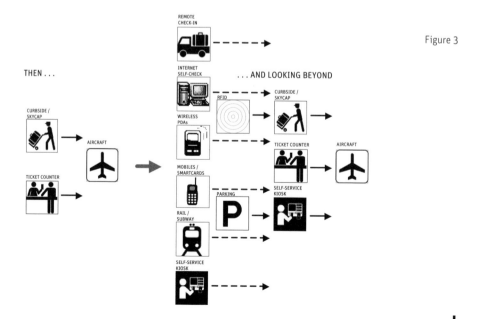

Figure 3

and changing performance requirements of a new paradigm for the 21st Century. Certain key questions must therefore be addressed in the immediate future that will leave an indelible mark on tomorrow's passenger terminal include:

How can passenger terminals return to the level of convenience that the air travel experience in North America once represented, especially when physical expansion may not be an option?

How will the deployment of technology applications ultimately transform passenger terminal space requirements, spatial practices, and airline operations? Will the frustrating process of going through a passenger terminal ultimately evolve into a seamless, yet concurrently more secure experience?

How can technology successfully serve as a surrogate for human interaction in a dynamic and highly customer service-oriented operating environment such as the airport? What are the passenger tolerance thresholds for technology applications and its lasting implication? How should airports and regulatory agencies strike the appropriate balance of convenience, safety, and privacy when handling sensitive passenger data?

How should passenger terminals build in flexibility to respond to evolving and highly specific user- and market-driven needs?

This line of inquiry, referred to as the NexTerm initiative, attempts to define the parameters of a new and responsive passenger terminal paradigm by effectively addressing these current-day challenges. Passenger terminals of the 21st century — both green-field and existing — must be increasingly responsive to and programmatically driven by the following factors:

CHANGING TRAVEL DEMOGRAPHICS AND NEW MARKETS—
Enhanced passenger-specific accommodations, where financially feasible, will determine airport and airline competitiveness. *One-size-fits-all* solutions to passenger terminals are less applicable when passenger sophistication increases and building programs diversify. Passenger duration of stay in the terminal and programmatic requirements will continue to vary and demand facilities that are capable of supporting this dynamic range (Figure 5).

As passenger characteristics continue to change, it is critical that the passenger terminal building keep pace. For example, as passengers continue to move in the direction of self-check and remote check-in, the convention of the ticketing hall may eventually be rendered obsolete (Figure 6).

EVOLVING REGULATORY REQUIREMENTS AND SCREENING PROCESSES
Information technology and systems integration will likely, as a matter of time, emerge as one of the most critical components in the initiative to improve the security screening of airport users to be more accurate, streamlined, integrated, and unobtrusive.

The Federal Aviation Administration's (FAA) current use of their existing Computer-Assisted Passenger Pre-screening System (CAPPS) software application has already raised some considerable concerns, particularly with privacy advocates

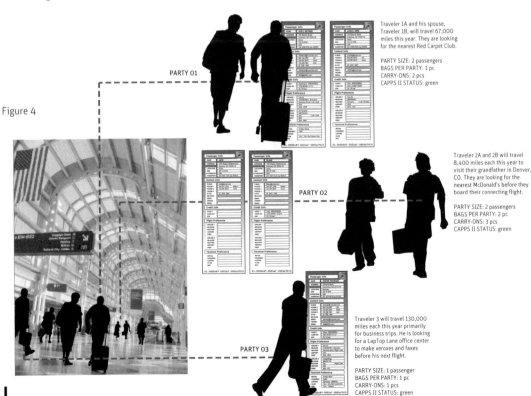

Figure 4

PARTY 01

Traveler 1A and his spouse, Traveler 1B, will travel 67,000 miles this year. They are looking for the nearest Red Carpet Club.

PARTY SIZE: 2 passengers
BAGS PER PARTY: 1 pc
CARRY-ONS: 2 pcs
CAPPS II STATUS: green

PARTY 02

Traveler 2A and 2B will travel 8,400 miles each this year to visit their grandfather in Denver, CO. They are looking for the nearest McDonald's before they board their connecting flight.

PARTY SIZE: 2 passengers
BAGS PER PARTY: 2 pc
CARRY-ONS: 3 pcs
CAPPS II STATUS: green

PARTY 03

Traveler 3 will travel 130,000 miles each year primarily for business trips. He is looking for a LapTop Lane office center to make xeroxes and faxes before his next flight.

PARTY SIZE: 1 passenger
BAGS PER PARTY: 1 pc
CARRY-ONS: 1 pcs
CAPPS II STATUS: green

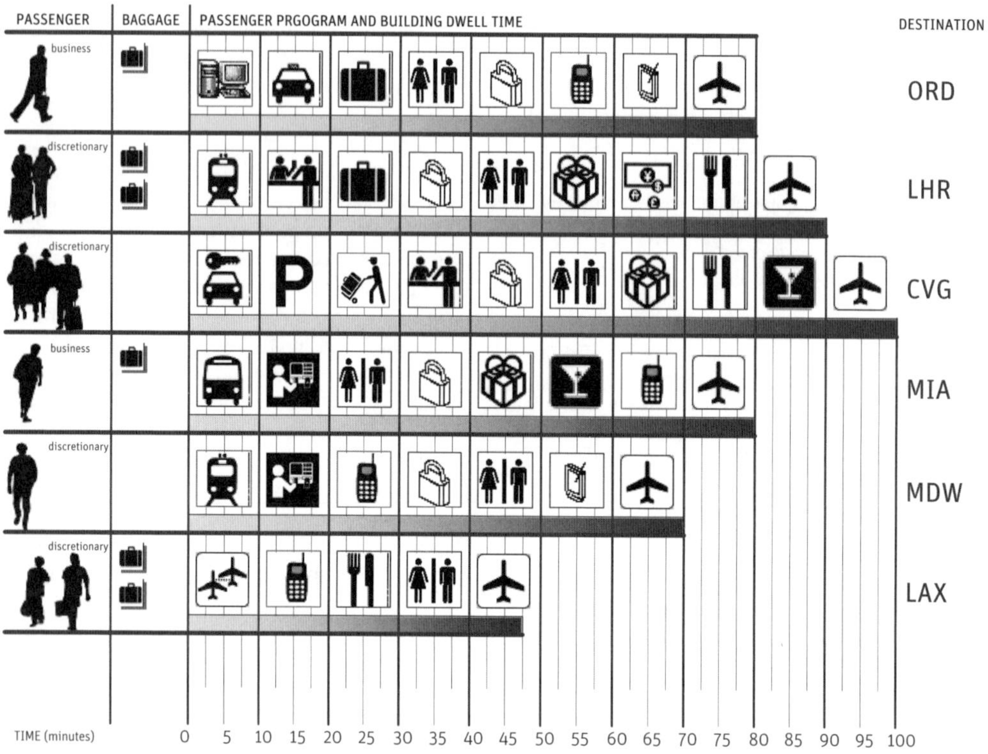

PASSENGER	BAGGAGE	PASSENGER PRGOGRAM AND BUILDING DWELL TIME	DESTINATION

Figure 5

over the FAA's criteria for identifying selectee passengers. The CAPPS application, tied to the airlines' ticketing reservations system, runs algorithms to determine a passenger's probability of posing a security risk during the ticketing process based on factors including the passengers' method of payment for their tickets, the type of tickets they purchase — one-way versus round-trip — as well as his or her travel history.[1] The new CAPPS II application will require every person on a commercial flight in and out of the U.S. airspace to provide four pieces of key personal information — full name, home address, telephone number and date of birth — when booking a flight. This data would be input into a network of commercial databases that would build a personal profile of the passenger to ascertain whether the passenger poses a security risk. Passengers would then be coded green, yellow or red, with the code encrypted on their boarding passes — based on the designated colors, passengers are either cleared to travel or will require additional security scrutiny. The new U.S. V.I.S.I.T. citizenship and immigrations inspection program will add a new dimension to the domestic passenger database with the introduction of biometric authentication, including the use of iris scans, facial imagery, and fingerprints, combined with a kiosk-based interface.[2]

Airports and regulatory entities are challenged with the difficult balancing act of providing thorough and comprehensive security with the realities of operating cost and public sensitivity.

How and where to detect, identify, and deter security threats remain unresolved and are severely contested issues, as there are currently no institutionally accepted methods to go by. However, it can be assumed that physical and database-oriented surveillance will continue to proliferate to enhance security. As such, airport operations can anticipate higher levels of passenger scrutiny — even before they ever set foot in the terminal — with a perceived sense of transparency or unobtrusiveness.

A non-airport example of rigorous, yet transparent security practices is the system currently used in the United Kingdom where the ratio of surveillance cameras to citizenry is approximately 1 to 15. As such, UK residents can expect to be captured on a security camera over 300,000 times a day. Public surveillance in the UK has become more than a function of security, it has been re-appropriated as part of everyday life. It even plays a day-to-day role in identifying parking and toll payment violators.

Air travelers, through time and political maneuvering, will be thoroughly identified, authenticated, and vetted as they enter the passenger terminal facilities with virtually no human interaction at the airport. Convenience, though, will not be without a cost. Striking that balance between convenience and the makings of an Orwellian infrastructure has become a major policy challenge in the latest evolution of the passenger terminal.

AIRLINE OPERATIONS AND FACILITIES OPTIMIZATION— Airlines are likely to continue pursuing technology applications as core solutions to enhancing overall facilities capacity and mitigating staffing and cost constraints. In addition, other approaches being tested to reduce the operating footprint of the ticket lobby include the deployment of RFID technology in the check-in process in which passengers and baggage are immediately identified and tracked upon entry into the airport system. As such, passengers can be checked-in by simply walking into the ticket lobby and authenticating their identity — using an ID card or biometrics — in seconds. The effective deployment of RFID and other decentralized check-in systems will significantly minimize the amount of fixed, dedicated areas generally required to process passengers, such as the check-in queue, and leave only the functional spaces truly necessary for passenger processing, such as baggage check-in, flight upgrades, or actual ticket purchases. With the successful deployment and recalibration of current technologies such as RFID, much of the dedicated space and lengthy wait times of the passenger check-in process may be eliminated, thus freeing up real estate, lease expenditures, and passenger wait areas for better uses.

Current technology applications showing promise in effectively decentralizing the check-in process, such as Personal Digital Assistants and Smart Cards, are being assessed to determine their ability to improve check-in options and enhance the passenger decision support options in and beyond the airport environment.

The evolution of self-service and staff optimization at airline ticket counters will both minimize spatial requirements and raise the question of how to better utilize airport space in the near future. Certain ticketing layouts (Figure 7) suggest an operation in which some ticketing space would no longer be required using RFID-based check-in. Airlines have unwittingly, through the inherent hassle of congestion in the ticket lobby, ticketing agent contact, and the option of self-service, developed a new customer service standard equating good service with no staff interaction. Should recent trends prevail — including the elimination of *paper* ticketing, full airline meal services — it may be just a matter of time before the entire airport experience becomes a wholly self-serve process.

Speculations for the Future

If form truly follows finances, especially in the airport development context, terminals of the future will continue to respond to the wave of change. The following ruminations consider some future possibilities for the airport passenger terminal.

GETTING TO THE AIRPORT WHEN YOU REALLY NEED TO— Instead of going to ticket counters and waiting indefinitely in ticketing and checkpoint queues, future passengers would likely be pre-notified of airplane delays and be assigned precise times to arrive at the airport and enter the queues. Future passengers will significantly benefit from improved real-time flight information and have the decision-making tools immediately at hand. Working with current real-time flight information notification tools, airlines can develop enhanced information systems notifying passengers as to precisely when and where they should arrive at the airport. As such, the time between leaving home and arriving at the airport will be vastly more synchronized and predictable — empowering passengers with more control over their time spent in the airport environment.

In the arrival experience in the passenger terminal, new and improved way-finding and communications tools for the passenger should be a key part of empowering passengers when entering the airport facility. Passengers should be able to immediately enter the appropriate facilities with limited confusion and wasted time. Perhaps passenger terminals can be reconceived with designated routes by terminal user characteristics, including:

Passengers with no bags to check-in
Passengers with bags to check-in
Passengers needing to purchase tickets
Group check-in
Passengers with special needs
Airport Meeter-Greeters and Well-wishers

For frequent travelers or technology-savvy travelers, current wireless, and PDA technologies could be tied in with airline communications systems to provide a virtual navigational interface for passengers — replete with location information, check-in and security processes and terminal-specific requirements, and other important processing information.

VIRTUAL CHECK-IN— Passengers arriving at the airport may no longer need to go through the check-in process as we know of it. Instead, future passengers, using RFID technology or alternative wireless technologies, would be immediately identified as soon as they enter the airport property. Their travel itinerary and individual passenger information could be immediately pulled up and confirmed upon entry into the system. Travelers would then be immediately identified and checked in as soon as they enter the passenger terminal. This process is efficient but not completely transparent as passengers, however, would be slightly hindered by the requirement to authenticate their identity using some for of biometric confirmation — either hand

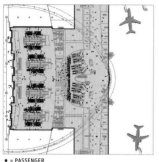

1999

CURRENT

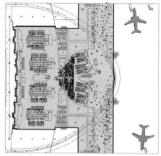

20XX

■ = PASSENGER

PASSENGER CHECK-IN OPTIONS AND DISTRIBUTION	
% TICKET COUNTER	80%
% CURBSIDE	15%
% REMOTE (HOTEL)	05%

Figure 6

PASSENGER CHECK-IN OPTIONS AND DISTRIBUTION	
% TICKET COUNTER	70%
% CURBSIDE	10%
% REMOTE (HOTEL/GARAGE)	05%
% KIOSK	10%
% INTERNET	05%

PASSENGER CHECK-IN OPTIONS AND DISTRIBUTION	
% TICKET COUNTER	40%
% CURBSIDE	05%
% REMOTE (GARAGE/HOTEL/METRO)	05%
% KIOSK	20%
% WIRELESS / RFID TECHNOLOGY	10%
% SMART CARDS / BIOMETRICS	05%
% INTERNET / PAN TECHNOLOGY	15%

geometry or iris scanning. Rather than continue with casual visual inspection of documents, biometric technology can offer a significantly more effective authentication process to ensure the identity of all travelers.

THE DECENTRALIZED TICKET LOBBY— The spatial impacts of new technology and applications may alter the footprint of conventional terminal buildings in such a way that traditional facilities — including as ticketing positions and checkpoints — may soon be eliminated altogether, should current technology deployment initiatives prove successful. As a consequence of the continued decentralization of the passenger check-in process, it may no longer be necessary for passengers to use the ticket lobby to obtain boarding passes and directions. And perhaps this evolution may ultimately free up the lobby and dedicate ticketing positions for the sole purpose of purchasing tickets and upgrading passengers. Consider the passenger terminal ticket lobby being reconfigured for better revenue generating uses, such as additional retail facilities, passenger amenities, and improved airline club rooms. Rather than using the ticket lobby for queuing, it could be better deployed for more productive uses.

TRANSPARENT PASSENGER SCREENING— As they are fully vetted — with the help of various middleware and information corroboration applications — upon entry into the airport system, passengers could be immediately identified — using the CAPPS database — as either cleared or passengers requiring additional secondary screening. If a passenger requires additional screening, they would be notified early on in the process with adequate screening instructions and location. With virtually no interaction, a passenger can be fully screened and have their relevant personal and travel data thoroughly vetted by TSA. While the appropriateness of such screening processes is being debated in the public arena, the refinement of such technology marches on.

Self-Service Airports?

These speculations into the future of commercial aviation facilities are not universally applicable to all airports. However, appropriate deployment of certain technologies and alternative processes may substantively enhance airport operations and meet their strategic objectives. Technology and its recent application to the airport industry's challenges of evolving markets, demographics, passenger privacy, regulatory requirements, and airline realities, only begin to reveal what may be to come in the second century of flight. Even with all the indeterminacies of relying on technology solutions, perhaps the self-service airport will remain the lesser of two evils. As *New York Times* technology writer, Amy Harmon, puts it:

> Rejected for decades as too complicated, the machines are being embraced by a public whose faith in technology has grown as its satisfaction with more traditional forms of customer service has diminished. Faced with the alternative — live people — it seems that many consumers now prefer the machines.[3]

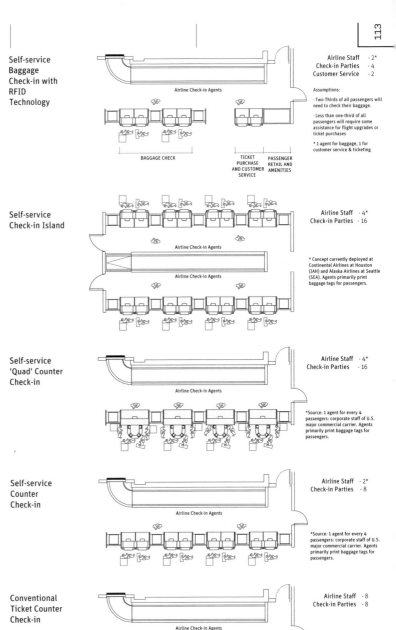

Self-service Baggage Check-in with RFID Technology

Airline Check-in Agents

Airline Staff - 2*
Check-in Parties - 4
Customer Service - 2

Assumptions:
· Two-Thirds of all passengers will need to check their baggage.
· Less than one-third of all passengers will require some assistance for flight upgrades or ticket purchases
* 1 agent for baggage, 1 for customer service & ticketing

BAGGAGE CHECK   TICKET PURCHASE AND CUSTOMER SERVICE   PASSENGER RETAIL AND AMENITIES

Self-service Check-in Island

Airline Check-in Agents

Airline Check-in Agents

Airline Staff - 4*
Check-in Parties - 16

* Concept currently deployed at Continental Airlines at Houston (IAH) and Alaska Airlines at Seattle (SEA). Agents primarily print baggage tags for passengers.

Self-service 'Quad' Counter Check-in

Airline Check-in Agents

Airline Staff - 4*
Check-in Parties - 16

*Source: 1 agent for every 4 passengers: corporate staff of U.S. major commercial carrier. Agents primarily print baggage tags for passengers.

Self-service Counter Check-in

Airline Check-in Agents

Airline Staff - 2*
Check-in Parties - 8

*Source: 1 agent for every 4 passengers: corporate staff of U.S. major commercial carrier. Agents primarily print baggage tags for passengers.

Conventional Ticket Counter Check-in

Airline Check-in Agents

Airline Staff - 8
Check-in Parties - 8

Figure 7

NOTES

1. Congressional Memo, *Subcommittee on Aviation Hearing on Aviation Security with a Focus on Passenger Profiling* ‹http://www.house.gov/transportation/aviation/02-27-02/02-27-02memo.html› ‹http://www.dhs.gov›. Released February 27, 2002.

2. Press Release, "Department of Homeland Security Unveils U.S.-VISIT Program" ‹http://www.dhs.gov/dhspublic/interapp/press_release/press_release_0286.xml›. Released October 28, 2003.

3. Harmon, Amy. "More Consumers Reach Out to Touch the Screen," *New York Times*, November 17, 2003.

Derrick Choi is a Senior Consultant and Terminal Facilities Planner with Leigh Fisher Associates, a division of Jacobs Consultancy, Inc. He has over five years of international and domestic experience in Airport Passenger Terminal planning, simulation, and design projects. He received his Bachelor of Art from Columbia University and his Master of Architecture from the Harvard University Graduate School of Design. His career interest in airport passenger terminal design and planning issues commenced with an internship in the New York office of Skidmore Owings and Merrill.

PLATIAL
PRACTICES

ALTERNATIVE INHABITATIONS FOR JFK

Patricia Acevedo-Riker

Many constructions of the everyday world — train stations, airports, hotels, shopping malls — are familiar from a connection, a fleeting visit or a few days stop. These are not spaces toward which visitors will normally feel an affinity, where they would feel at home, or where they might meet other people. Rather, visitors are chaotically thrown together. Commercial transport buildings are, in their most basic form, transit and service spaces visited in varying lengths of time — in-between spaces. These spaces lack meaning as *places* in the classic anthropological sense because visitors don't feel any attachment to them. In anthropological terms, a PLACE is an area that has acquired social meaning as a result of human activities. "Places want to be — people want them to be — places of identity, of relations and of history."[1]

"Places to which people do not feel any special attachment and which do not function in a conventional manner as meeting places are *non-places*."[2] "*Non-place* designates two complementary but distinct realities: spaces formed in relation to certain ends — transport, transit, commerce, leisure — and the relations that individuals have with these spaces."[3] Non-place is not the opposite of place, but rather it is a new type of place. Not all non-places lack social meaning — some provide for inhabitants to have relations with the territories, their families and others — *i.e.* Grand Central Station, NY, Dulles International Airport, DC.

Globalization has subjected the individual to new experiences and ordeals of solitude, creating neither singular identities nor relations with others, only loneliness and similitude. Non-places immerse the mobile consumer in a sea of anonymity, while at the same time requiring proof of positive identity — passport, credit card, pin number. Users share a common need to be fulfilled, creating a homogeneous body from individual identities that are not inclined or invited to relate to each other. Non-places are interchanges to be passed through, thus they are generally measured in units of time.

> Numerically, the airport is situated at the extreme end of a transport-junction scale, which also contains bus terminals, railway stations, and motorway service stations. That is, places where qualities emerge from quantities.
>
> —Ben Van Berkel, Caroline Bos[4]

pla·tial [adj.] relating to, occupying or having the characteristics of place.

average
household
income $79.000

access mode
air 33%
private car 28%
taxi 15%

residence
local 32%
other u.s. 38%
foreign 30%

originating +
terminating 67%
transferring 33%

age
25-34 25%
35-44 22%
45-54 21%
average 41yrs

female 47%
male 53%

business 25%
personal 75%

Social scenario

Non-places have defined their own vocabulary: they have created a reference point for commercial and generic transit spaces. Non-place building typologies — bus stations, train stations, airports, motorway stops, hotels, office buildings, supermarkets, shopping malls, leisure parks — are made up of basic elements, used over and over again, as building blocks in different permutations to fit each new location. This propensity toward large-scale repetition is augmented by the design of non-places, generally ruled by tight technical analyses and logistical standards to work out functional spatial relationships and generate layouts. In the end, most results are experientially similar; the language of airports is so similar, that ubiquitous services and goods can be found, regardless of the specific location, in predictable places for those en route.

> A foreigner lost in a country he does not know — a passing stranger — can feel at home there only in the anonymity of motorways, service stations, big stores and hotel chains.
>
> —Marc Augé[5]

As these non-places proliferate, the uniqueness and loyalty to the history and identity of the locale is overlooked. These spaces are located in a specific setting, but they have a generic makeup that stimulates a rejection of what surrounds them. In the same seemingly hygienic manner, they relate to the user by words and symbols: their instructions for use establish the traffic conditions of spaces in which individuals are supposed to interact only with signs.

By their presence and life in the urban scene, and attachment to the country or city they inhabit, these so-called non-places have become places. Today the agents that shape place are dependent on different conditions than those that shaped place in the past. No longer does the vernacular inform these places: the specific conditions of the locale — economics, climate, religion, available materials and technology, history and culture — don't dictate the aesthetics of *non-places*. Instant data-access, mobility of goods and people, new information technologies and the permitting economy are major factors in the development, spread and success of this new type of placement. Changes in the way people travel and the effects of globalization have repercussions for the way non-places are shaped, programmed and perceived, creating situations where non-places become a new kind of place: the mega-space. Non-places have become a certain system of landmarks in the cities they inhabit, a sort of citywide branding. These spaces are rooted to their cities by becoming familiar images over time. It might be said that today, place is based on interpersonal interaction, personal interaction with a space, local self-expression for individuality and the orchestration and acceptance of time variables and local needs.

The elegance and the exclusivity that was once attached to flight in the jet age is forgotten; millions of tourists think nothing of flight in a jet airliner, as it has become an everyday phenomenon. National borders and time zones are no longer barriers to interchange; boundaries seem to have eased, until recently, as the climate of fear caused in large part by September 11th, 2001 has permeated commercial air travel. Recent changes have called for harsher security measures, affecting the redefinition of the domestic and international boundaries inside the airport, making the passenger's captivity obvious. Travelers now, more than ever, require and demand a welcoming and sympathetic environment.

airports

	organization	pax / yr	flights/yr	movement	ownership	split domestic : international
1 ATL atlanta. us		80'171'036	915'454	15'997	city of atlanta dept of aviation	76:24
2 ORD chicago. us		72'135'887	896'110	16'156	department of aviation. chicago	76:24
4 LHR london. uk		64'477'689	451'373	8'618	british airport authorities. baa	6:94
8 CDG paris. fr		48'240'137	459'691	8'321	aeroports de paris	8:92
10 AMS amsterdam. nl		39'604'589	396'627	6'647	schiphol group	2:98
20 JFK new york. us		32'779'428	343'327	4'501	panynj	35:65
22 HKG hong kong. cn		32'747'737	180'191	3'218	airport authority of hong kong	0:100

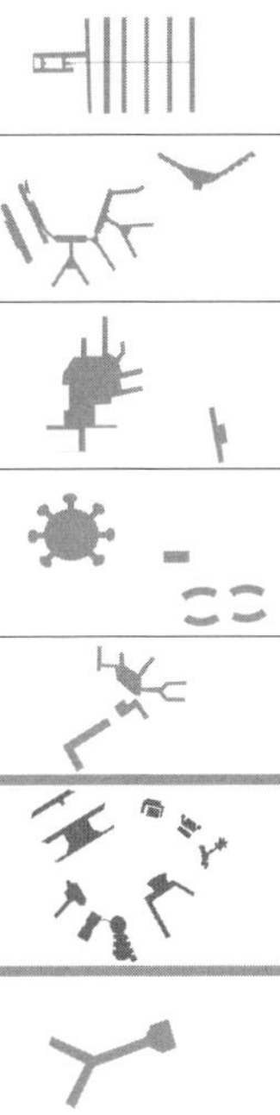

Terminal city vs. megaterminal

inhabitants [i]

traits [t]

0 variants	↑PBT	↑PBT	↑PBT	↑PBT	↑ PBTI	↑ PBTI	↑PBTI	
1 variant	↑pBT	↑pBT	↑pBT	↑pBT	↑ pBTI	↑ pBTI	↑pBTI	
	↑PbT	↑PbT	↑PbT	↑PbT	↑ PbTI	↑ PbTI	↑PbTI	
	↑PBt	↑PBt	↑PBt	↑PBt	↑ PBtI	↑ PBtI	↑PBtI	
					↑ PBTi	↑ PBTi	↑PBTi	
2 variants	↑Pbt	↑Pbt	↑Pbt	↑Pbt	↑ Pbt I	↑ Pbt I	↑Pbt I	
	↑pBt	↑pBt	↑pBt	↑pBt	↑ pBt I	↑ pBt I	↑pBt I	
	↑pbT	↑pbT	↑pbT	↑pbT	↑ pbTI	↑ pbTI	↑pbTI	
					↑ pBTi	↑ pBTi	↑pBTi	
					↑ PbTi	↑ PbTi	↑PbTi	
					↑ PBti	↑ PBti	↑PBti	
3 variants	↑pbt	↑pbt	↑ pbt	↑pbt	↑ Pbti	↑ Pbti	↑Pbti	
					↑ pBti	↑ pBti	↑pBti	
					↑ pbTi	↑ pbTi	↑pbTi	
					↑ pbt I	↑ pbt I	↑pbt I	
4 variants					↑ pbt i	↑ pbt i	↑pbt i	

16 profiles   16 profiles   48 profiles

80 profiles

traits [t]

citezenship
P u.s. passport holder
p non_u.s. passport holder

check_in
B no bags checked
b bags checked

timing
T non_peak time
t peak time

transfer
I inter_terminal
i intra_terminal

inhabitants [i]

↑ originating domestic
↑ originating international
↑ terminating domestic
↑ terminating international
↑ transferring port of entry
↑ transferring port of exit
↑ transferring in_transit

Inhabitational profliing

With the massive growth and popularization of flight, airports have become cities. In their basic state, airports are defined by their clarity — the efficiency with which they deliver passengers. Airports are not only a threshold between land and air, but are also systems that isolate us from the rhythms of the world. At the same time, airports don't communicate how the artificial world of global aviation works.

> . . . airports no longer serve isolated functions. They are not unitary buildings; they extend and redefine the metropolis; they explode boundaries and limits.
>
> —Bernard Tschumi[6]

Airports are the only space that many people experience in a city; while waiting to get on a connecting flight, people experience the space of the airport without necessarily seeing or engaging with the city they are in. The specifics of the airport seem to be reduced to local branding, while the services provided — the shops and food stops — are chains repeated from airport to airport, bringing global branding into the mix.

Today airports work by slowing people down for consumption purposes while at the same time becoming inclusive of other non-places. What used to be comprised of terminal buildings, control tower and runways has grown significantly due to increased pre-flight times, flight delays and connection times, leading to the inclusion of everything from hotels, shopping malls, movie theatres and train stations — basic services now provided to and expected by the airport occupant.

Kennedy International Airport (JFK) is considered a *place* via its unique city-airport relationship, its significance in the country's immigration, visitors and travelers' collective memory, and for its inimitable design. When it began its commercial services in 1948, JFK was ready for the jet age, having been designed for — then — anticipated needs, far from what the world had seen. It offered the traveler a glamorous lifestyle that accompanied travel vis-à-vis aesthetics and technology. The concept of a terminal city was embodied by the master plan for JFK: several independent terminals, in which each terminal had its own architectural style and belonged to a different major airline or group of airlines. Sixty years after its completion, JFK is no longer a viable solution for the needs of airlines and travelers. It has confronted major problems in keeping pace with the fast growth of the air transport network, in part due to the lack of space for airport expansion and the decentralized ownership of the terminals.

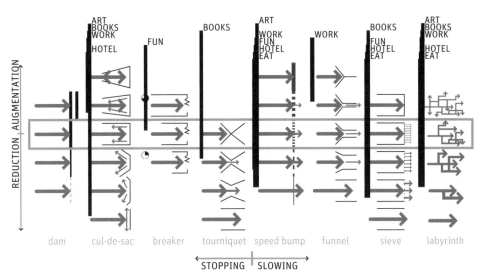

REDUCTION — AUGMENTATION

ART
BOOKS
WORK
HOTEL

FUN

BOOKS

ART
WORK
FUN
HOTEL
EAT

WORK

BOOKS
FUN
HOTEL
EAT

ART
BOOKS
WORK
HOTEL
EAT

dam   cul-de-sac   breaker   tourniquet   speed bump   funnel   sieve   labyrinth

STOPPING | SLOWING

Flows + resistances

flexible_space   wired   crew_zone   threshold   b o h   ctrl_space   quiet_space   loading   food_prep

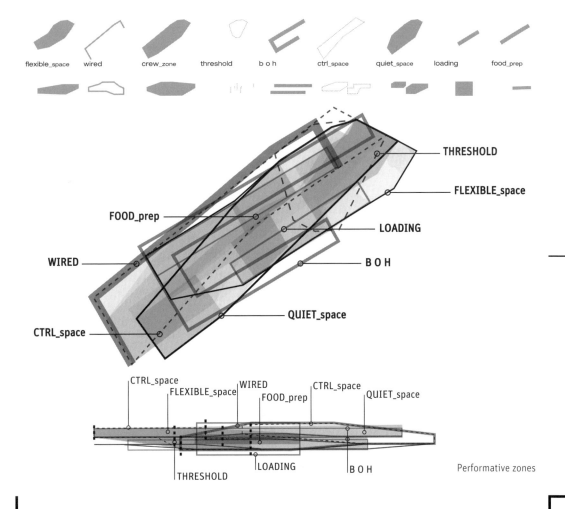

THRESHOLD
FLEXIBLE_space
FOOD_prep
LOADING
WIRED
B O H
QUIET_space
CTRL_space

CTRL_space
FLEXIBLE_space
WIRED
FOOD_prep
CTRL_space
QUIET_space
THRESHOLD
LOADING
B O H

Performative zones

One good thing that JFK has for itself is that the architecture accurately depicts the present chaos of the air travel system. Privately owned terminals, managed by individual air carriers, arranged to emulate a world's fairground of national pavilions.

—Herbert Muschamp[7]

The effects of globalization, advances in technology, permitting economies and the ease and popularity of air travel have made the concept of the terminal city obsolete. It has led to the megaterminal — i.e. Kansai, Schiphol — a new response to the contemporary idea of flying and growing air travel needs. Megaterminals generally consist of continuously sweeping spaces, with reconfigurable interiors, consisting of interchangeable kiosks — airlines and brands — that respond to instabilities of the air transport network; business models transform and airline carriers constantly appear, disappear and merge.

... Airports are much more than boarding or transfer places. An airport is like a city a dynamic traffic hub where people and business, logistics, shops, information and entertainment meet. Like in a city, worlds come together at an airport. Wherever worlds come together, direction is needed, which connects, integrates and goes beyond the different elements of that airport city.

—Vision: Schiphol Group[8]

Alternative inhabitations emerge when the airport system of passenger flows becomes overstressed, as unscheduled overflows and surges build pressure that must be relieved. TerminaLink will join existing terminals, accommodating new inhabitational patterns and strengthening the existing airport infrastructure through a new circuit of internal airport exchange. Two parallel rings of services and extras serve airside and landside, as connections between terminals. The links direct the flow of travelers, but also create a field of stresses and resistances, provoking the travelers to explore a range of inhabitational possibilities. The mobile, though captive, variable volume of passengers inhabit the airport for varying durations of time, choosing programs and levels of service and social interaction.

The terminal city lacks coherence as a model for travel in the twenty-first century. TerminaLink enables the traveler to impart coherence on the seemingly scattered system by deciding to "hit, activate, configure or simply bypass the various spaces."[8] As such, the introduction of a more comprehensive program will provide alternatives to the degeneration of the airport into a shopping mall. Challenging this degeneration and accepting JFK's inevitable alignment to the concept of megaterminal, TerminaLink engages both the obsolescence and the idiosyncratic qualities of the terminal city in offering new models of tactical inhabitation within the global air travel network.

Patricia Acevedo-Riker holds a Master of Architecture from Rensselaer Polytechnic Institute and a Bachelor of Science in Environmental Design from the Universidad de Puerto Rico. Her experience includes graphic and architectural design with MateriaLab in Troy, NY on projects including the Imagining Ecologies Symposium and their finalist entry in the 2001 PS1 Young Architects Competition: Paradise Island. Currently, Patricia works at Spencer, Maxwell, Bullock Architects in Pensacola, Florida as an architectural intern and graphic designer.

Patricia completed Platial Practices as her Masters thesis at Rensselaer Polytechnic Institute, with David Riebe as thesis advisor. Ken Warriner and Jefferson Ellinger were reviewers.

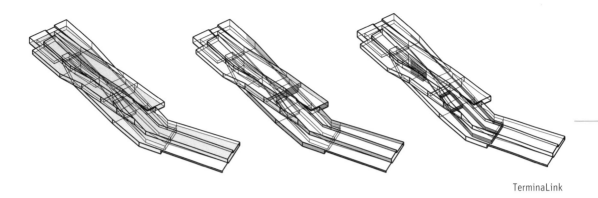

TerminaLink

NOTES
1. Augé, Marc. *Non-Places: Introduction to an Anthropology of Supermodernity.* London/New York: Verso, 1995.
2. Ibelings, Hans. *Supermodernism: Architecture in the Age of Globalization.* Rotterdam: NAi Publishers, 1998.
3. Ibid, Augé.
4. Van Berkel, Ben and Caroline Bos, "Radiant Synthetic Effects." *Anything.* Cambridge: MIT Press, 2001.
5. Tschumi, Bernard. "Passing Time In Space, Airports and the Urban Phenomena." *Anything.* Cambridge, The MIT Press, 2001.
6. nARCHITECTS http://Www.narchitects.com
7. Muschamp, H. "JFK Enters The Era Of The Megaterminal." *The New York Times.* 19 March 2000.
8. Amsterdam Airport Schiphol <http://www.schiphol.nl>

Vintage photographs of JFK Airport courtesy of Mary Ann Riker. Photographs in montage courtesy of the Associated Press.

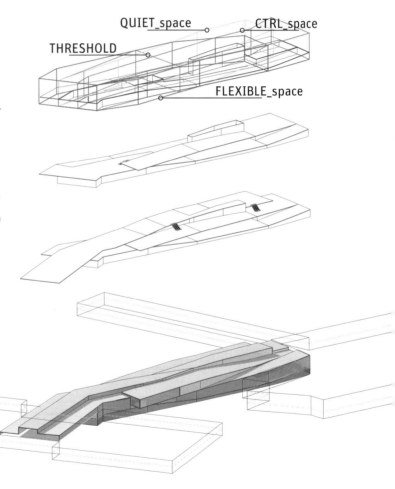

QUIET_space   CTRL_space
THRESHOLD
FLEXIBLE_space

A SPACE FOR
THE NATION

THE CAPITOL CENTER IN THE NATIONAL IMAGINATION

Jess Wendover

A Space for the Nation: The Capitol Center in the National Imagination

> Architecture and its symbolism are never so closely wed as to prohibit divorce and eventual remarriage.
>
> —Lawrence Vale[1]

While architecture everywhere serves to communicate abstract symbolism, the two are seldom more closely joined than in the commission of government designs. Every building and space is the result of a bold move on the part of an architect, an agency, or a leader. The resulting spaces are then re-cast for public consumption on postcards, in government publications, and as backgrounds for television news broadcasts.

Governments and the architects they employ frequently use the space of the capitol center in the active construction of a national identity. As often as not, the lived, on-the-ground experience of these capitol centers is not coterminous with the government's intended meaning.

While governmental efforts to spatially employ the capitol center are often driven by a desire to assert political control over a populace, the spaces of the capitol center are more frequently employed by non-governmental actors. These popular activations of governmental space demonstrate that the social effects of governmental architecture can be positive or restorative, as well as repressive.

Media Constructions in Tiananmen Square

> You can tell a lot about a country by the kind of building it has.
>
> —President Harry Truman[2]

Tiananmen Square, now an infamous example, illustrates that true representation is not an inherent aspect of public space. What makes the square truly significant to this discussion is its role in an international construction of national identity. The Square was designed as a place for crowds to witness displays of power by the government. Tiananmen, like every square in the People's Republic of China, conjoins with a platform from which leaders address the people and review the mass assemblies. Mao Zedong, the first leader of Communist China, addressed members of the Red Guard in the Square. The tremendous Square can accommodate crowds of up to one million people and was designed for such sizable public assemblies, but never as a discursive space.

On April 17, 1989, the Square became the locus of the internationally covered student protests for democracy. Students gathered to mourn the death of communist leader Hu Yaobang, who had expressed tacit support for allowing opposition to the Party. Hu had once told a national newspaper that, "Marx and Lenin can't solve our problems."[3] In order to protect the wreaths, posters, and memorials to Hu, the students illegally stayed overnight in Tiananmen. Four weeks later, when the police came to disperse the students, the international media, who had been in town to cover Mikhail Gorbachev's conference with Chinese leader Deng Xiaopeng, turned their cameras on the growing student-police conflict in Tiananmen.

The Square was so large that the students could not cover all of it with their demonstrations, so they quickly gathered in areas where the international news cameras were filming. The students wrote lists of demands in English and held them before the cameras, cognizant of the language of choice among potential international viewers of the footage. A group of young researchers painted a banner that read, "Satellites reach heaven but democracy is stuck in hell."[4]

The government of modern China is housed in the massive Great Hall of the People on the edge of Tiananmen Square. During Gorbachev's visit in 1989, an official dinner was held in the Great Hall, where immense drapes were closed to block panoramic views of Tiananmen Square and the student protests. Citizens and visitors can take free self-guided tours of the building every weekday, but the tour only allows access to various ceremonial meeting rooms. Indeed, on a recent visit, not a single pen or piece of paper was visible in the publicly accessible portion of the building. Such secrecy surrounding the workings of upper level Party decisions is not surprising to observers of modern China; one international observer notes, "everything that is known about the way politics is conducted at the highest levels suggests that flattery, friendship, nepotism, and favoritism count far more than policies or ability."[5] In contrast with the large and open Square, the Great Hall of the People is designed to allow for strict spatial control.

The international media's focus on the student protests in the Square, and indeed the students' decision to locate their protest there, are driven by a Western conception of a public space as a requisite for modern democracy. But in modern China, the power of Tiananmen Square for dissenters or journalists is over-ridden by the hulking and inaccessible architecture of the neighboring Great Hall of the People, the site of most closed-door functions of the government.

Reclaiming the Government Spaces of Apartheid

The word decolonization has not yet acquired an agreed definition.
—John D. Hargreaves[10]

Though blacks had been segregated from white populations under British rule in South Africa, not until 1948, when the Afrikaaner government took power, were the segregation rules of Apartheid instituted as national policy. Despite a volatile national history of race relations that includes the forcible removal of over three million blacks from cities to overcrowded and peripheral urban townships or remote rural settlements, a spirit of reconciliation pervaded the transition to post-Apartheid government in South Africa. This attitude allowed for a relatively peaceful transition between governments and an uneventful appropriation of the colonialist architecture of the Capitol buildings in Cape Town and Union Buildings in Pretoria.

Architects, planners, and urban designers were in a peculiar position: the Apartheid government used their medium — urban space — to reinforce racial divisions. The Apartheid state exerted control over a wide variety of municipal functions to achieve complete physical, economic, and social segregation and to subordinate less advantaged groups. Many architects who were hired by the state to build projects in this atmosphere "kept quiet and did their work."[7]

The starkest physical remnant of apartheid planning is the duplication of public amenities and an unnecessarily large bureaucracy. The 1953 Separate Amenities Act called for distinct schools, halls, swimming pools, and recreation facilities and was essential to viability of the broader Group Areas Act, which called for general residential segregation. In addition to general inefficiency, by neglecting economies of scale, the redundant infrastructure is often unequally apportioned: facilities in white communities are often underutilized, while those in black communities are overburdened. The separate facilities also mask the economic integration of the races: by the mid 1980s, many blacks worked in mid-level or managerial positions, and the black share of cumulative economic power was growing.

Resistance to these planning practices was largely initiated on a grassroots level: residents in the black townships organized street committees around individual issues regarding everyday quality of life. In some cases, the scarcity of public facilities in black areas — like water taps — led to street violence, as warlords mobilized squatter settlements to maintain access to facilities in the nearby formal townships, and groups of township youths organized military-style units to protect township facilities from squatter use. This type of internecine violence in black areas predominated in the 1980s and 1990s, while many white suburban areas were immune to rising levels of violent outbreaks. Continuing outbursts of violence in the townships rendered it difficult for any of the African political movements to mobilize mass demonstrations and showed the necessity of a politically negotiated settlement to end Apartheid.

The government of P. W. Botha in the mid 1980s had attempted previous efforts at neocolonial compromise. In a 1984 effort to incorporate black allies, the constitution weakened the white minority rule by bringing Colored and Indian representation into the main house of Parliament. Such schemes for coopting African collaborators proved ineffective. By the time the government of F.W. De Klerk took over in 1989, there was little alternative but to collaborate with the main nationalist movement, the African National Congress (ANC), which had overwhelming international legitimacy and a majority support at home.

After the adoption of an interim constitution in 1994, Nelson Mandela, leader of the ANC and the president after the first nationwide democratic elections, expressed sympathy for the desire of the Afrikaaners to retain their language and culture and invited them to participate in negotiations to argue their case for an Afrikaaner homeland. DeKlerk, leader of the National Party, had lambasted conservative whites during the last session of the apartheid Parliament by arguing that there was no future in upholding demands for the unobtainable dream of an autonomous white homeland. In this political atmosphere, Mandela's respectful treatment of the Afrikaaner homeland plan manifests an attitude of great accommodation of the outgoing Parliamentary structures by the new leadership of the ANC.Mandela even went so far as to adopt the symbols of the National Rugby Team, formerly a bastion of the country's white-dominated sports, by donning the captain's jersey and running onto the field to cheer the team in its World Cup Championship match in 1995. The nearly all-white crowd cheered "Nelson! Nelson!"[8]

This evolutionary method of transition, based on compromises and peaceful adoption, represented for many Africans a *selling out* of the revolutionary cause for which the liberation struggles had been fought. A lack of transformation in other areas, such as the nation's economic system, indicates that the change in governments may represent little besides power transferal from one elite to another, from white colonial rule to black majority rule. The new government has become an even firmer advocate of liberal capitalism than its predecessor.

The Mandela government used space to great effect in the political transition from Apartheid. Besides the successful adoption of previously white symbolism in the space of the media, Mandela also embraced the physical spaces of the struggle over Apartheid in order to confront the painful attachments of history. The Union Buildings in Pretoria house the national administrative headquarters, and the expansive garden in front of them was the site of an August 1956 protest by 20,000 African women who stood silently outside

the building for thirty minutes, waiting to deliver a petition to the empty prime minister's office. For his inauguration ceremony, Mandela selected this same garden in front of the Union Buildings, and the unprecedented size of the crowd allowed to assemble there gave a new definition to the contested space.

The consolidation of the three separate capitals of South Africa is a persistent topic of national debate. The issue touches on South Africa's conflict-ridden colonial and apartheid past: when Britain united the country as one colony in 1910, after defeating the independent Afrikaaner republics in the Boer War, it agreed to create three capitals to pacify the losing side. Parliament went to Cape Town, while Pretoria became home to government administration and Bloemfontein received the Supreme Court.

Pretoria is the executive capital, and consolidation there would save the cost of government officials having to commute the 1,600 km (994 miles) to Cape Town during Parliament sessions. The selection of a possible unified capital at Pretoria or in nearby Midrand involves political and economic intricacies: these two sites are in the industrial heartland of the Gauteng Province, an ANC stronghold. Cape Town is in Western Cape, the only province to support DeKlerk's National Party in the 1994 election. Moving Parliament to Gauteng would punish Western Cape by depriving it of an estimated 861 million Rand a year ($131 million in 2003 dollars) in economic activity and 8,700 jobs spawned by the legislature. According to news reports, civil servants in Cape Town have been ordered to hold off on buying property until the final decision.

The South African Houses of Parliament in Cape Town were modeled on the Westminster system of Great Britain. The Victorian style building and surrounding gardens are an overt remnant of their colonial construction. The main Parliament building was completed in 1885 and became the seat of the national Parliament when the Union of South Africa was formed in 1910. In front of the building is a marble statue of Queen Victoria, erected in honor of her golden jubilee.

The Parliament Building was the site, in 1948, of the National Party's rise to power and the beginning of the racial segregation of colonial society to benefit Afrikaner descendants of Dutch settlers, and that history taints Cape Town's image. Many blacks link the Parliament complex with the hated apartheid laws and remember how they were never represented in the chamber until 1994.

A mere 80 feet away from the northern wall of the Parliament House sits the South African Cultural History Museum. The museum is housed in the second oldest existing building in South Africa, which was originally constructed as a Slave Lodge for the Dutch East India Company in 1679. Today, in addition to art and artifacts from around the world, the museum presents several displays about the building's former role in the slave trade.

"Tourists are always surprised that it's so close to the Parliament," said one museum historian, "but for us, that's just the way our country is."[29] Undoubtedly, the national attitude of reconciliation over the ills of apartheid allows a comfort with this physical proximity of the center of national legislative government and such a painful reminder of the nation's colonial history. The physical spaces of government in South Africa maintain a malleable identity. Due to active policies of appropriation like Mandela's choice of office location and the opening of the Slave Lodge Museum next to the Parliament, the physical spaces of government have transcended the intents of their original designers. With recent immigration of blacks from neighboring countries like Zimbabwe and emigration of whites to Australia, Britain, Canada, New Zealand, and the United States, the images of post-Apartheid Union Buildings and Parliament are adapted to meet the needs of a shifting population.

Adopting Louis Khan's Dhaka

> He wanted to be Moses here. It was nothing, only paddy fields, and you are going to build something that is going to be the best building in the world?
>
> —Shamsul Wares, professor of architecture in Dhaka[10]

The National Assembly Building at Dhaka is the best example of the way that the work of an internationally-renowned, or brand name architect can contribute to the construction of a national identity through buildings. The complicated political history of the commission for the project provides a unique opportunity to study the effects of Modernist architecture is a political setting for which it was not designed.

Louis Khan received a commission to design an assembly building for the second capital of Pakistan in Dhaka in 1962. In his design, he sought a framework that could relate new institutions not to their post-colonial stage in history, but to a more lasting, idealized representation. After spending nine years on the project, the commission was cast into turmoil: Khan's initial client for his building complex at Dhaka was the government of Pakistan, with its national capital in west Pakistan at Islamabad. The Dhaka complex was intended to serve as the functionary and administrative capital of the East Pakistan region, allowing Islamabad to exert control over the distant territory. During the civil war in 1971, Khan's contract was terminated and construction halted, but Khan continued his design work anyway. After the war, East Pakistan declared its independence and became Bangladesh. The newly independent nation-state decided to continue with Khan's design, using the complex as the national capitol instead of as a regional administrative center, as it was originally intended. One would expect the citizens of Bangladesh to attach a stigma to a building sponsored by the government against which they fought a civil war. But the architectural abstraction of Khan's Modernist design shortened the memories of the building's originally intended meaning, as expressed in the groundbreaking ceremony of the building, where huge crowds shouted their loyalty to the government of Pakistan. "Khan has found an elementary form which should be permanently acceptable."[11]

The occupation of Khan's complex by the nascent Bangladeshi government provides a model for the appropriation and transformation of a design logic. Most of the shifts in the meanings and names of symbols in the building are gradual changes and haven only been accomplished with the passage of time. For instance, Bangladeshis frequently paint images of the building on the aluminum panels of their jitney carts or boats. The building has risen to the status of national symbol, despite its design by a foreign architect and its original commission by a foreign occupying power.

Many aspects of the original design that were intended to foster control of the colonial citizens still function to affect the imperfect practice of democracy in Bangladesh today. Access to the capitol complex is rigorously controlled: the building is set in a moat and accessible only by one narrow bridge from the plaza in front of the complex. The government sells annual fishing permits to working class families that allows them to fish in the very artificial body of water that divides them from the center of their government. (The money collected from the permits funds a lounge where legislators play billiards.)[12] This practice, along with the much-needed open space that the Assembly's gardens provides, allows the government to re-cast a structure of colonial control in a beneficent light. But the realities of the building's control-oriented design foster undemocratic practices in Bangladesh.

Building Aboriginal Identity in Canberra

Following the federation of the British colonies of Australia in 1900, there was a movement to create a uniquely Australian, postcolonial national identity in the former colonies. The national capital at Canberra was established following a 1912 international design competition, won by the American architect and landscape architect Walter Burley Griffin. From the very beginning of the competition, and through the present day, the urban space of Canberra has been hotly contested. I will set aside the controversies surrounding Canberra as a compromised location between Sydney and Melbourne and the controversy between a tempestuous Griffin and the Australian government

to discuss the contest of the public spaces of Canberra in the struggle for Aboriginal identity in the Australian government. The garden in front of the *old* Parliament house and the entry plaza in front of the *new* Parliament, play a crucial role in understanding the Aboriginal Identity movement in Australia.

The Australian Parliament remained housed in Melbourne until the 1927 completion of the provisional Parliament House at Canberra. The provisional building is designed in an imported European colonial style, and overlooks a neatly manicured lawn.

By 1965, the provisional Parliament House was becoming too crowded and inadequate for its purpose. At the same time that the federal government began to focus on the design and construction of a new *permanent* Parliament House, indigenous Australians were actively forming a pan-aboriginal Australian identity. The new, more militant Aboriginal activism was inspired by the Black Power movement of the United States. The referendum of 1967 had shown the Australian public's overwhelming desire to "include Aboriginal people in Australian Society and civil life."[13]

Since the 1930s, Aboriginal Protection legislation in each state and territory forbade Aboriginal people from moving freely around the country without a permit and placed aboriginal children under departmental control. The most striking misinterpretation of pre-European inhabitation of Australia was reflected in the legal standard of terra nullius. For European legal purposes, it was considered that Australia, before European settlement, was "practically unoccupied, without settled occupants or settled law." The principle of terra nullius was legally overturned, only as recently as 1992, as a result of the Mabo ruling. Since that decision, the law now cautiously concedes that Australia was previously inhabited, indeed occupied. The Mabo decision, in principle, is profoundly significant for the ongoing process of reconciling present day Australia with the legacy of the Aboriginal Protection laws.

On the national holiday, January 26, 1972 — known alternatively as Australia Day or Invasion Day — four activists, planted a beach umbrella in front of the temporary Parliament House. Later that day, the protest for land rights for Aboriginal Australians evolved into a larger tent encampment and came to be known as the *Aboriginal Tent Embassy*.[14] The camp comprised a group of shelters made of assorted of materials including canvas and plastic tarps. The tent embassy capitalized on international media attention. The ephemeral quality of the embassy allowed it to appear and disappear suddenly; its mobility and portability aided its dramatic removal and re-erection after police crackdowns.

The Australian Heritage Commission placed the Aboriginal Tent Embassy on the register of the National Estate in 1995. Whereas permanent building may have been illegal under Building By-Laws, camping on the site in the Capital Territory in 1972 was not illegal. After the tent Embassy was erected in January 1972, it took until July 20 for the government to pass an ordinance to make camping on the grounds of provisional Parliament illegal, so that the police could use force to remove the protesters. Only then did Police demolish the Embassy in the "most violent demonstrations Canberra had ever seen," drawing international attention to the protest. The Canberra Times referred to an incident in which a passing driver called out to the Tent Embassy staff "Go home niggers, you've had your fun" whereupon someone replied "We're home, baby — you go home."[15] The visibility of the domestic reality made the Tent Embassy a more powerful symbol of the bleak, rural environment of many Aborigines. The "cooking in the open and bed linen spread out to dry" was reported as "bringing the reality of Aboriginal Australia right to Australia's front door."[16] The *Tent Embassy* appropriated the language of camping and the great Australian Outdoors. Rather than presenting a romanticized impression of nomadic life *in the bush*, the Embassy was actually an embarrassing reflection of the realistic contemporary dwelling conditions found in many fringe dweller camps in rural towns around the nation.

The process of choosing which of the competing group identities to be included in a single national identity is decidedly political. An example: the government design for the New Parliament House, completed in 1988, located near the old building, includes a public art project at the entryway that represents of the Aboriginal people's relationship to the earth. This architectural gesture was intended to subsume the dissenting Aboriginal identity within a broader multicultural identity, but the design is criticized as a figurative exclusion of the Aboriginal identity by incorporating it into an exterior portion of the building.

Jess Wendover is a community designer at Urban Ecology in Oakland, California. Her work involves neighborhood planning and architectural and urban design on behalf of low-income communities in the San Francisco Bay Area. This essay is based on her research under the 2002 John K. Branner Travelling Fellowship from U.C. Berkeley, where she earned her Master of Architecture and Master of City Planning.

NOTES

1. Vale, Lawrence. *Architecture, Power, and National Identity.*
2. Quoted in: Craig, Lois. *The Federal Presence: Architecture, Politics, and Symbols in United States Government Building.*
3. Wark, McKenzie. "Tiananmen Square, Beijing: Seeds of Fire." *Virtual Geography.* Indiana University Press: Bloomington, IN, 1995.
4. Ibid.
5. *The Economist.* "Out With The Old, In With The Old." November 9, 2002.
6. Hargreaves, John D. *Decolonization in Africa.* Longman Press: London, 1988.
7. Le Roux, Hannah. "Undisciplined Practices: Architecture in the Context of Freedom." *Blank___ Architecture, Apartheid And After.* Nai Publishers: Rotterdam, Netherlands, 1999.
8. Lyman, Princeton N. "South Africa's Promise." *Foreign Policy.* Spring 1996.
9. Interview with Lucy Campbell at the South African Cultural History Museum. March 2002.
10. Nilsson, Sten. *The New Capitals of India, Pakistan, and Bangladesh.* Curzon Press: London, 1975.
11. Nilsson, Sten. *The New Capitals of India, Pakistan, and Bangladesh.*
12. Interview with Mohammad Abu Dawood, Deputy Director of the Bangladesh Parliament Secretariat. August 2002.
13. Goodall, H. *Invasion To Embassy: Land In Aboriginal Politics In New South Wales,* 1770-1972, Allen & Unwin Publishers: St. Leonards, New South Wales, Australia.
14. Austin, Greg. "Aboriginal Flag Flies In Canberra." *Sydney Morning Herald.* January 28, 1992.
15. Waterford, J. "We're Already Home." *Canberra Times,* 1992.
16. Ibid.

RESIDUES OF WAR

Kathleen Heike Triem

War Rooms

On April 30, 1975 a Viet Cong tank crashed through the gates of Saigon's Reunification Palace, ending the existence of the American backed Republic of Vietnam. The palace, as it stands today, is a monument to that singular moment and testifies to the fleeting nature of the excesses of power.

One senses the hasty abandonment and the devastating psychological legacy of the conflict. Everything remains in its place as it was on the day the war ended. In the basement, a complex of tunnels and war rooms stand waiting for operation. Desks, maps, old teletypes and dial telephones provide an historic record of recent tragedy.

Technology provides an historic record as sources of cultural identity can be traced through its remnants. As the race of history accelerates through the Modern, technology becomes obsolete at an exponential rate. These photographs record a passage of only 30 years, yet the depicted scenes are charmingly obsolete. Time and history seem exponentially compressed. Memory no longer remains viable, rather, the only reality we process is the immediate sensorial *now*.

Surveillance Series

There is a fundamental tension in society between the forces of conformity and the desire for individual expression. The illusion of identity is something we confront on a daily basis from our professional to our emotional needs and aspirations.

The surveillance series critiques the cultish narcissism of the individual by removing the unique subject from focus. The images are derived from photographs taken by the artist at an intersection in Shanghai. Through a process of smearing heavy oil stick across the transferred image, the particular quality of the original becomes only faintly recognizable and hauntingly elusive. Specific characteristics are suppressed. We are left to behold only a generalized condition, not a unique instance.

The series explores tense relationships between a unique subject and generalized conditions in our built environment. Recent technologies, such as self-publishing, internet blogging and other communication tools, enable the voice of the individual, yet this overload of communication simultaneously overwhelms specific identity. The blurring of images in the series challenges the forces of homogenization in the environment.

Kathleen Heike Triem is a partner in F:T Architecture + Interiors, a firm exploring interrelationships between art and architecture. She is a photographer and co-Curator of The Fields Sculpture Park at The Art Omi International Arts Center in Ghent, NY.

OKAY NEWS

Rebecca Ross in collaboration with
Matthew Rothenberg and Brendan Kenny

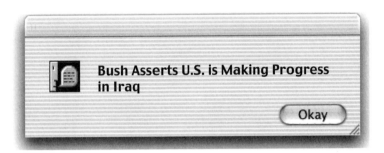

Bush Asserts U.S. is Making Progress in Iraq

Okay

Rebecca Ross lives in Brooklyn, New York. She teaches design at New York University's Gallatin School and is a Researcher at the NYU Center for Advanced Technology. Rebecca received a Master of Fine Arts from Yale School of Art in 2002. Her thesis, *Handling Distance* dealt with relations between authority and symbology. Rebecca currently works on improving structures for public participation in maps.

The *Okay News* is a re-formed newspaper that runs as memory resident software in the background of everyday computer use. Every twenty minutes it delivers a headline from that day's New York Times to an operating system warning box with the single button "Okay." The news must be approved to continue using the computer. This interface is an explicit embodiment of the implicit approval most of us issue by choosing to remain uninvolved.

Many established conventions of information delivery make users or readers comfortable with their lack of concern for and participation in the meaning being delivered. Along with a bagel and a warm cup of coffee, the *New York Times* maintains a stronger association with a comfortable Sunday morning at home than a means of connecting individuals to difficult events of national and global concern. The tropes of newspaper design, the narrow columns and familiar typography, distance us from being empathetic while making us feel as if we are somehow engaging responsibly with its subjects.

Similarly, the standardization of graphical user interface elements homogenize content by consistently associating the same forms with diverse functions and content. We use the same ten abstract interface widgets to check out movie times, buy our groceries and express our deepest feelings to friends and lovers. Just as our culture goes to great lengths to pack realistic detail into films and video games, it goes through great pains to protect itself from stirring deep feelings toward current events. The *Okay News* attempts to demystify and question this process.

The *Okay News* is available for download at http://famousmime.com/okay/.

DYNAMIC EFFECTS
IN AN ARRESTED
STATE

Warren Neidich

Warren Neidich's photographs of noise barriers draw attention to the fact that signs, overwhelmingly understood as semantic, have material manifestations as well. The enlarged text, high contrast, and simplified graphics of expressway signage are designed to be effective along corridors of extreme velocity and heightened risk. These material dimensions signify the nature of the expressway independent of any narrative content. The expressway itself is not a zone defined by signage; rather, the road and its signage are both regimented by material logics. In fact, restrictive signage along the highway is essentially imperative, offering minimum direction to the driver in a necessarily reductive language, in accordance with a simplified zone; their material register of speed is more relevant as an admonition of behavior than their semantic content. The real restrictions of the road, after all, are material.

An appropriate analogy is to the old sign at the end of the runway: "If you can read this sign, consider yourself dead!" Any pilot who did read this was flying either too low or too slow, and wasn't going to make it.

These corridors are derived neither from phenomenology nor from linguistics, at least as an interpretive discipline. In this dynamic milieu, there is no time to perceive — save in the most reduced form — as there is no time to interpret, save as is necessary to make the most rudimentary choices.

This amounts to an argument for a different conception of material and information. Under certain conditions, no amount of data can supersede the reality of the ground rushing up at you, or the effects of vehicles rushing past. Planning disciplines have long recognized this argument and sought to separate expressways and the subdivisions of exurbia. Noise barriers are among the new material arrangements that have been developed to deal with these old adjacencies, accommodating overlapping needs as settlement patterns grow denser and traffic volume continues to increase.

These noise barriers relate less to the pedestrian politics of race, class and gender than to human survival in the corridor. The overwhelming issue from within the vehicle is transmitting and reacting to information as quickly as possible. The noise barriers are information; they are ordering terms within the envelope of velocity, sensory instructions converted into material and action at speed. The barriers only become interpretive signs when converted to art as photographs or when encountered spuriously in a static or arrested state, on foot.

The noise barrier, a resolution of the material reality of noise pollution encountering the environmental engineering of the subdivision, is to a sign that reads *do not honk* as a concrete median is to a sign that reads *do not enter*. The noise barrier is an after-effect of scales that exceed the human, in the case of the highway: the turning radius of a standard vehicle, the width of a lane of traffic, the friction co-efficient and reverberative properties of concrete that define a range of highly restricted material flow. While the noise barriers are not formed with traditional sculptural values in mind, they have consequential effects that produce them, especially when rendered in the static sublime of photography.

Jesse Reiser

Warren Neidich is currently an ACE-AHRB fellow of the British Council for the Arts and artist in residence in the department of Visual Arts at Goldsmiths College, London. *Silence: A State of Being*, his collaborative sculpture, is currently installed on the Paseo de Castellana as part of Madrid Abierto. He is author of *Blow-up: Photography, Cinema and the Brain*, recently published by DAP and the Ford Foundation. He is currently working on *The Neuro-Aesthetic Reading Room*, a travelling reading room which will first be shown at the Burea Freidrich in Berlin.

Jesse Reiser is a Principal of Reiser+Umemoto RUR Architecture PC in New York, and Assistant Professor of Architectural Design at the School of Architecture, Princeton University.

SWITCH SITES

Emily Eastman

Building flexibility into our infrastructure will be one of the key challenges of this century. The character of the entire national economy is shifting, as manufacturing yields to the rising service sector, and as computers and advanced communication technologies revolutionize the production, consumption, and distribution of goods and services. It is difficult to predict exactly what kinds of infrastructure will be needed to provide the technological sinews of the future, but to be guided by nostalgic ideas about reconstructing the infrastructure of the past would be a terrible error. Only a flexible system that responds to changing market signals can effectively provide for this new era.

Interstate Highway

Between 1890 and 1960, the American highway system was transformed from two million miles of poorly built, disconnected roads into a coordinated system of four million miles of paved roads. During these years the focus of American highway policy also changed from farm-to-market roads to a federally aided system of roads between cities. In 1956 this culminated in the creation on the Interstate system, a 41,000-mile network of limited access expressways.[1]

Although the Interstate Highway System was designed as an intercity network, some earlier experiments and proposals treated the highway as a long-distance transcontinental route that bypassed cities and interfaced terrestrial networks as well as other forms of conveyance like the railroad. Redundant or coincident organizations potentially facilitated interface among rail, water, and highway not only for inter-modal exchange but also for network specialization.

Original plans called for bypassing cities in an effort to provide long-haul interstate travel; it was not planned for the local commuter traffic we see today. By the time the plan was implemented in 1956, however, beltways and arterials were extant. These forerunners of the Interstate system encouraged suburban development. Shortly thereafter, automobile congestion and urban sprawl began, nurtured by our federal highway program.[2] The Interstate system thus became an inter-city network layered on a pre-existing intra-city network of highways. This resulted in highways diverging from the railroad outside the city and coinciding with it inside the city, reducing their potential to develop a variety of ex-urban ports of exchange outside the city.

Redundancy

The issue for almost two centuries of infrastructural development has not been whether to build, but how. Our bureaucrats, however, have never produced a coherent infrastructure policy. This lack of developmental coordination between transportation modes has created a widespread system of overlapping corridors and networks, including canals and piers, passenger rail, working and abandoned freight rail, mass transit, surface streets and expressways. These redundancies have been quite destructive in the past, generating a transportation philosophy which put modes in competition with one another, creating inefficiencies and rigidities.

Like the redundancies that are intentionally built into an electronic network to amplify its intelligence, these overlapping corridors and networks potentially support a kind of parallelism that, through connection, could strengthen our transportation infrastructure. Many of the redundancies among transportation networks have developed through cycles of replacement and supposed obsolescence, unaccompanied by a deliberate process of selection and recombination that would build parallelism in the network and better match carriers to transportation needs and tasks.

The separate networks that have developed from the fight for dominance between water, rail, highway, and air have laid the groundwork for a potentially intelligent, combinatorial network that allows for interchange. As such, sites of redundancy could be developed as switch sites of differential exchange among carriers, since joining one complex network to another potentially increases their combined intelligence. Unlike a binary switch with only two positions, these switch sites would perform as a differential, allowing more continuous translation between modes to regulate or modulate the entire transportation network.

In order to begin to locate these redundancies as potential locations for switches between transportation modes, a national map of these overlapping networks was developed. The map includes interstate highway, rail, navigable waterways, and air travel routes. The map effectively locates zones of redundancy among our transportation systems which can be classified into three types: linear, edge, and node. In addition to carrying its own set of physical characteristics, each of the three types carries specific implications regarding the appropriate scale at which to understand these sites.

Zones that emerge as linear conditions of redundancy — such as the corridors between St. Paul MN and Milwaukee, WI; and between Albuquerque, NM and Los Angeles, CA — are quite

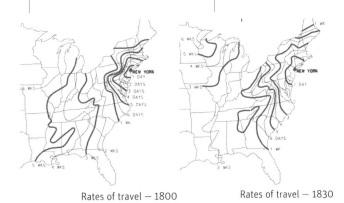

Rates of travel — 1800

Rates of travel — 1830

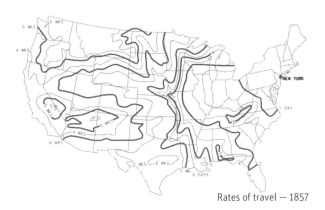

Rates of travel — 1857

Rates of travel — 1930
(by airways)

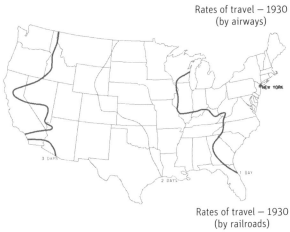

Rates of travel — 1930
(by railroads)

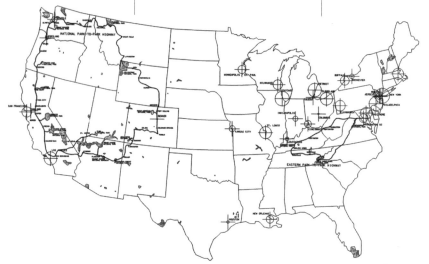

Park to park highways — 1930

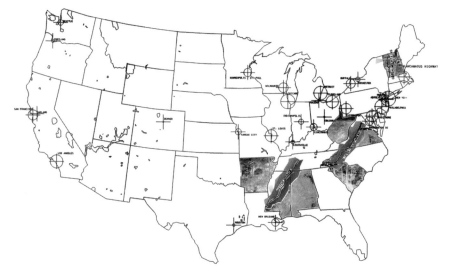

Skyline drives — 1934

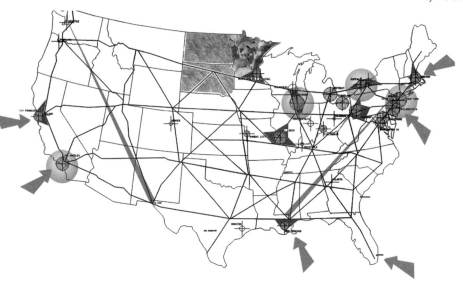

National motorway plan — 1939
Norman Bel Ceddes

large. However, the nature of their redundancies can be revealed only by selectively zooming in to scales unique to each site.

Edge conditions — such as Jacksonville and El Paso; and node conditions — such as Memphis, Salt Lake City, and Pittsburgh — must also be understood at a unique set of scales. The task of understanding each switch site becomes impregnated with the complexity of its simultaneous operation at multiple scales.

In classifying the nature of redundancy, two types of redundancy seem most prevalent among transportation networks:

a physical redundancy: two modes are physically parallel but not competing against each other to provide identical services

an operational redundancy: two modes are in competition to provide an identical service, but are not physically in parallel, responding to the limitations of each mode.

Understanding the physical aspects of redundancy is merely one side of the issue. Redundancy is not a matter of sheer adjacency; it is also a condition of programmatic redundancy. Currently, the overlaps and redundancies in the existing transportation systems are indicative of modes in competition with each other to provide a particular service.

The multi-scalar operation and design of SwitchSite, is an attempt to make the modes more continuous as one network — not a series of systems in competition with one another. As such, SwitchSite focuses on the location of physical redundancies and then attempts to locate the programmatic opportunity. This entails an understanding of the services provided by each system — or zone of the system — involved and using SwitchSite as a means to create a richer, smarter, more continuous network.

The underlying operation of SwitchSite is continuous translation, thus it cannot be designed as a static entity, but rather is designed to operate in various states. This suggests that the method for designing SwitchSite is rooted in the design of various states that are then performed in a sequence or in response to specific conditions. The translation is an exchange that relieves some kind of existing tension on the site. It occurs at the location of a pressure.

The Tipping Point

Like any condition that is loaded with tension, the zones of redundancy between modes of transportation have potential to be *tipped*. The theory behind the performance of SwitchSite is rooted in epidemiology.

The best way to understand the emergence of fashion trends, the ebb and flow of crime waves, the transformation of unknown books into best sellers, the rise of teenage smoking, or social word-of-mouth phenomena is to think of them as epidemics. Ideas and products and messages and behaviors spread just as viruses do. That one dramatic moment when everything can change all at once is the Tipping Point, a point at which an extremely small action can have a disproportionately large effect.

The best way to understand the Tipping Point is to imagine a hypothetical outbreak of the flu. Suppose that during one summer 1,000 tourists come to Manhattan carrying an untreatable strain of a twenty-four-hour virus. This strain of flu has a 2% infection rate, which is to say that one out of every 50 people who come into close contact with someone carrying it catches the bug himself. Let's say that 50 is also exactly the number of people the average Manhattanite — in the course of riding the subways and mingling with colleagues at work — comes into contact with every day. What we have, then, is a disease in equilibrium. Those 1,000 tourists pass on the virus to 1,000 new people on the day they arrive. And The next day those 1,000 newly infected people pass on the virus to another 1,000 people, just as the original 1,000 tourists who started the epidemic are returning to balance, the flu chugs along at a steady but unspectacular clip throughout the rest of the summer and the fall.

But then comes the Christmas season. The subways and busses get more crowded with tourists and shoppers, and instead of running into 50 people per day, the average Manhattanite now has close contact with, say, 55 people per day. Suddenly, the equilibrium is disrupted. The 1,000 flu carriers now run into 55,000 people per day, and at a 2% infection rate, that translates into 1,100 cases the following day. Those 1,100, in turn, pass their virus on to 55,000 people. By day three, 1,210 Manhattanites have the flu, and by day four 1,331. By the end of the week there are nearly 2,000, and so on, in an exponential spiral, until Manhattan has a full-blown flu epidemic on its hands by Christmas day.

That moment when the average flu carrier went from running into fifty people per day to running into fifty-five people was the Tipping Point. That is the point at which an ordinary and stable phenomenon — a low-level flu outbreak — turns into a public health crisis. If one were to draw a graph of the progress of this 24-hour flu epidemic, the Tipping Point would be the point on the graph where the line suddenly turns upward.[3]

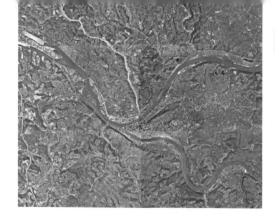

We can imagine how fashion trends and rumors may act like epidemics, but how is SwitchSite like an epidemic? SwitchSite is located at the site of extreme tension between redundant transportation networks. If we think of this condition as a tipping point, the Switch is the small action, at the right place and the right time, which sets a series of events into motion. The Tipping Point may seem like an unpredictable condition, but despite its instability it is possible to anticipate and predict possible outcomes and behaviors.

SwitchSite intends to operate at the Tipping Point of several systems. Through its performance as a transportation switch, SwitchSite is poised to *tip* interconnected systems such as economic conditions, urban development conditions, ecological conditions, and industrial conditions. It is these systems that will register changes disproportionate to the Switch.

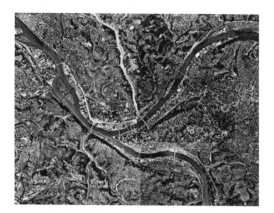

Just as SwitchSite is being developed at multiple scales, the nature of tipping must be understood at various scales as well. At the scale of the linear condition, it is possible to understand tips in regional economic conditions that are based on fluctuations in industry. The transportation aspect of SwitchSite has profound implications for the economical transport of goods across the country. These long, linear corridors between cities that are linked by industry are layered with transportation redundancies and loaded with tension, in terms of intermodal competition. This competition is driven almost completely by economics. With SwitchSite poised to have significant impacts on the efficiency of economy transport, the performance of these industrial corridors is seen as a tip-able condition.

At the scale of the edge condition, the large-scale industrial and economic conditions may become invisible, but conditions related to leisure travel and commuter traffic become visible. Again the transportation aspect of SwitchSite has potential to profoundly effect the nature of everyday commutes to work and the nature of pleasure travel. However, these are conditions that would not be understandable at smaller scales, but would be revealed at larger scales.

At the scale of the node condition, it is possible to understand a tip in social conditions at the scale of a neighborhood or household. The economics and entertainment characteristics of a neighborhood can also be understood at this scale and can be considered tip-able.

Sites

SwitchSite would be developed at multiple scales simultaneously, each scale informing the context of the others. The node condition would be developed most specifically, while the edge and

linear conditions are developed as strategies for deploying the Switch at their various scales. The site chosen to represent the linear condition is the corridor between Milwaukee, Wisconsin and St. Paul, Minnesota; the site chosen to represent the edge condition is Jacksonville, Florida; and the site chosen to represent the node condition is Pittsburgh, Pennsylvania. Mapping redundancies is not intended to locate existing switch sites, but to locate sites loaded with potential for switching. Intensely redundant sites are seen as such opportunities.

The distance between Milwaukee and St. Paul is about 330 miles and takes about six hours to drive. The industries along this corridor are grain, oil seeds, fertilizers, scrap steel, scrap aluminum, salt, construction aggregates, coal, cement, heavy machinery, and asphalt. This corridor is dominated by economy transport between the port of Milwaukee on the Great Lakes and the port of St. Paul, on the Mississippi River. SwitchSites are deployed at 55-mile intervals — placed with approximately one hour of driving time between them — along the main routes between the two cities. In this way SwitchSite can begin to modulate the continuous translation of goods between these two cities. At this scale SwitchSite provides potential for smarter, more economical, inter-modal transport between these two port cities. In addition, this strategy has significant urban development implications in the immediate areas around SwitchSite. Many of these locations are in under-populated areas. SwitchSite begins to mark these locations as destinations: as such, SwitchSite may develop into a small town or community, supported by the economics of the Switch.

The one-hour interval between the St. Paul-Milwaukee SwitchSites — and the economic outgrowths enabled by SwitchSite — begin to determine the characteristics of the Switch at each location. For example, at Hour 1, a hotel may not be necessary, but a café and restrooms may. Meanwhile, the Switch at Hour 1 is also Hour 5 driving from the opposite direction, and may be Hour 8 of another network of Switches. SwitchSites, deployed across a long, linear scale, have the potential to tip economic and development environments through a transportation Switch.

Jacksonville is characterized by its three international ports and its tourism industry. Its main exports are groceries, beer, poultry, autos, meat, and paper. Thus the transportation environment is dominated by the city's presence as a global port. These exports come from regions surrounding the city via various modes of transportation, and are distributed to one of Jacksonville's three ports. The commuter network dominates the transportation environment within Jacksonville. It operates in a

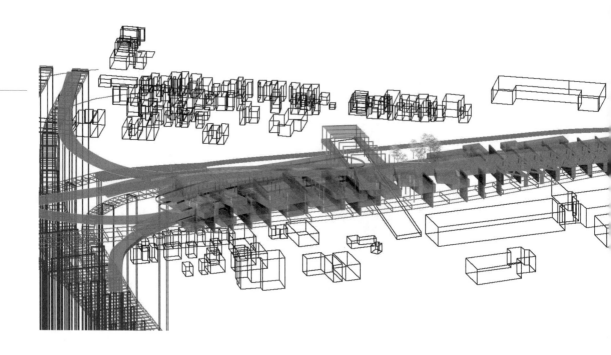

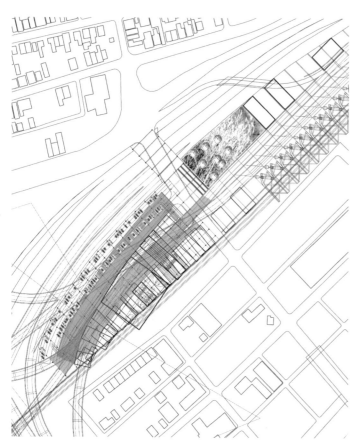

Emily Eastman, Assoc. AIA, attended
Rensselaer Polytechnic Institute, receiving
a Bachelor of Architecture, Bachelor of
Science in Building Science, and a minor in
Transportation Engineering in 2001.

She joined Richard Dattner & Partners
Architects in July 2001, where she is
currently involved in a number of projects
relating to transportation infrastructures,
including the Number 7 Subway Extension,
the Myrtle-Wyckoff Station Rehabilitation,
and develops proposals for prospective
projects for New York City Transit.

Ms. Eastman serves on the Board of
Directors at the AIA/New York Chapter,
representing non-licensed architects. She
has served as the chair of the Emerging NY
Architects Committee. Her work has been
published in the Journal of Architectural
Education.

SwitchSites was developed as a
Bachelor of Architecture thesis project at
Rensselaer Polytechnic Institute. It was
advised by David Riebe and reviewed by
Dr. George List and Anna Dyson.

NOTES

1. Keller Easterling, *Organization Space:
   Landscapes, Highways, and Houses in
   America.* Cambridge, Massachusetts:
   The MIT Press, 1999.
2. Bruce Seely, "The Saga of American
   Infrastructure", *The Wilson Quarterly.*
   Winter 1993.
3. Malcolm Gladwell, *The Tipping Point:
   How Little Things Can Make a Big
   Difference.* Boston: Little, Brown and
   Company, 2000.

similar fashion to the industrial network, gathering
commuters from the outlying areas and the beaches
and distributing them to the downtown area. The
strategy for SwitchSite at the urban periphery
is for it to perform as a gateway to the city. It
is strategically positioned at several key access
points to the city. At these points, goods and
passengers are Switched to a mode appropriate
for their destination. Commuters may Switch to a
commuter rail system and goods may Switch modes
appropriate to the specific port destination and the
characteristics of its access.

The Pittsburgh site is characterized by
an intense condition of redundancy between
highway, freight rail, and under-utilized navigable
river. Here, SwitchSite also has the potential
to take on a smaller-scale social concern, in a
local neighborhood. A major highway built in the
1980s divided the neighborhood into two parts,
both of which have become quite depressed
areas. SwitchSite has the potential to reconnect
these two neighborhoods — socially as well as
economically. In terms of developing SwitchSite in
a more detailed, specific way, this site was given
greater attention than the Jacksonville or St. Paul-
Milwaukee corridor because of its physical scale and
the scale of its social and economic characteristics.

By selecting sites, through the method of
locating them as sites of infrastructurally operative
redundancy within a national context, each site can
be understood as an element of a possibly national
network of SwitchSites. Developing SwitchSite at
multiple sites allows the Switch to be understood at
different and multiple scales — as part of regional,
city-wide, and neighborhood systems, as well as at
the national level.

ABOUT WAYS AND DRIVE-THRU LIFE

Lynne Opper

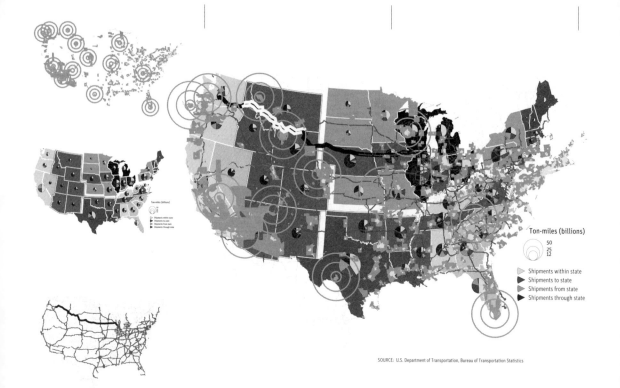

Ton-miles (billions)
50
25
12

▷ Shipments within state
▶ Shipments to state
◁ Shipments from state
◀ Shipments through state

SOURCE: U.S. Department of Transportation, Bureau of Transportation Statistics

The pioneering spirit that drives Americans to claim and make space is nearly as strong as the capitalist spirit that compels Americans to claim and make money. Americans value spatial abundance and *platial*[1] security. The gated yard and set back homes, typical of suburban development, embody these values spatially.[2] The phenomena of sprawl and *megaburban*[3] growth are the results of these values interacting with strata of federal funding and infrastructure.

The Interstate Highway system is the predominant and most extensively pervasive form of *public*[4] transportation infrastructure in the United States. The implementation of this system has allowed for an urban population migration to the suburban frontier. Therein, spatial proximity and economic ties are maintained with urban centers and coupled with comparatively abundant space. The Interstate allows for vehicular distortion of temporal and spatial proximity between town and country, city and suburb, dirty and clean, dangerous and safe.

The Interstate Highway system has a reputation, foremost, as a connector of places and a developer of open spaces. It is also the largest public works project ever undertaken by the Federal Government. As such, its roughly 40,000 completed miles comprise the largest and most linear civic space. Ways of life have not only grown from and around, but have also grown within the framework of the Interstate Highway system. Its inhabitants live normalized lifestyles rooted in the often transient and occasionally long term engagement of this functional civic space. To these inhabitants, the Interstate is known as home, office, and backyard.

Place within infrastructure is a different type of landscape, activated daily along the Interstate Highway System by a variety of participants. In this uniquely American landscape, the development of certain contemporary lifestyles and dependence on vehicular mobility — and the ways in which the roadways are inhabited — has laid claim to and redefined sites adjacent to those infrastructural systems. This redefinition and reclamation has no physical expression — yet — because of the rigor with which the system was engineered an executed as a national transportation and defense network. When the extensiveness of the system is taken into consideration, along with the amount of time it takes to drive 3,000 miles — a coast to coast long haul: 3,000 miles at 60 mph equals 50 hours, or 2 days driving time — the infrastructure becomes a space that is not only enacted or engaged during the act of driving but also inhabited for days and weeks at a time as a means of leisure travel, transport, and employment.

Where has the corporate development of this American landscape left the driver? Currently, the inhabitants of the Interstate Highway system rely largely on tactical shifts between various exchange structures, in order to secure amenities associated with having a permanent or fixed place. Chain service providers are the only entities that can function profitably within, and take advantage of, the scale encompassed by this national network. Within this network, divers are drawn to the light of the golden arches perched atop 50 foot poles located near access points.

The efficiency and scale of the Interstate system are utilized strategically by nationally cohesive entities. Food and service chains thrive adjacent to on- and off-ramps. Whether Americans truly enjoy biggie-sized-super value-combo-deluxe-luxury desserts is hard to say. Maybe it's just easiest because it's on the way. Food and service chains easily adapt and grow to compete on a national level as site requirements such as a busy intersection can easily be upgraded in scale to include interchanges. Strategic placement is one of the keys to success for service industry corporations.

Drivers, particularly through-travelers, must rely on signage to indicate placement and brand names, and to testify to quality when they decide to stop and claim temporary home space. When drivers stop on the Interstate system they are in one of two situations: they may be in a pocket of federally or state owned — commercially developed — land designated as a service area; or they may be in a zone that exists adjacent to a system access point, at the periphery of the Interstate system. Periphery zones are developed in an ad-hoc manner as chain service providers — and developers of the *oasis* type travel plazas, such as The Flying J® and Travel America® — compete for territory at a national scale. Currently, these commercial entities comprise most of the national-local interface for goods and people at the Interstate Highway system's accessible edges.

The types of commercial and infrastructural service establishments designed for drivers are *People Parking Lots*. People Parking Lots assume many forms, ranging from the fast food restaurant to campgrounds on state and national land preserves. They file vehicles into tidy rows or wandering loops, depending upon length of stay and the nature of the establishment.

People Parking Lots are a temporary home space for those who drive. The vehicle as a private space inhabits a spot or site, defining it as taken or occupied. The activities that occur within the private space of a vehicle are only restricted by its scale and options package. Two particular types of

People Parking Lots are truck stops and recreational vehicle campgrounds, in which the driver is identified by motor vehicle type, defining them as trucker or RV-er.

The theoretical development of Active Stops is a response to the corporate way in which the Interstate has been conquered and claimed. In contrast, the older U.S. Highway system often lacks homogenous zoning, allowing for situations of localized control, which creates potential for more romantic, rambling journeys.

The American landscape, from the perspective of the Interstate, is engineered quite well for the physical act of travel. Culturally, however, it is quite bland. "When we get these thruways across the whole country, as we will and must, it will be possible to drive from New York to California without seeing a single thing."[5] This is due to the clearly defined local and national edge that the interstate presents physically and economically.

"When the forces that facilitated the legislation of the Interstate Highway system merged with the agendas of commerce and defense, all claims to pioneering individualism were subsumed into one of the most centrally controlled and bureaucratically directed chapters in American history."[6] The Interstate is rife with potential for parallelisms and negotiations of both terrain and resources, leading to a character not considered in the planning of a thorough of rapid transit network.

The condition of the line or edge of the Interstate has two different, distinct identities: one as toll road, and one as freeway. On the East Coast, many existing toll roads were adopted into the Interstate system and allowed to remain tolled, although the Interstate was originally conceived of as a freeway. Toll roads charge by distance traveled along them and provide basic facilities via service areas; these isolated pockets of commercial activity are accessible only to automobiles. Freeways are also limited-access, but leaving the wayside to fulfill service and rest needs is not penalized with a fee or toll.

The western half of the U.S. is rife with business loops — parallel roads that have multiple access points to and from the Interstate system. These roads are lined with large-scale commercial entities, such as car dealerships, as well as gas stations, fast food restaurants and the types of industry that caters to through-travelers. Business loops serve as a connector to the highway, but also to local commercial entities. Business loops feed from both sides of the national and local edge that the Interstate highway has developed and now enforces.

"People Parking Lots"
Typologies in National Networks
Analysis of performative components

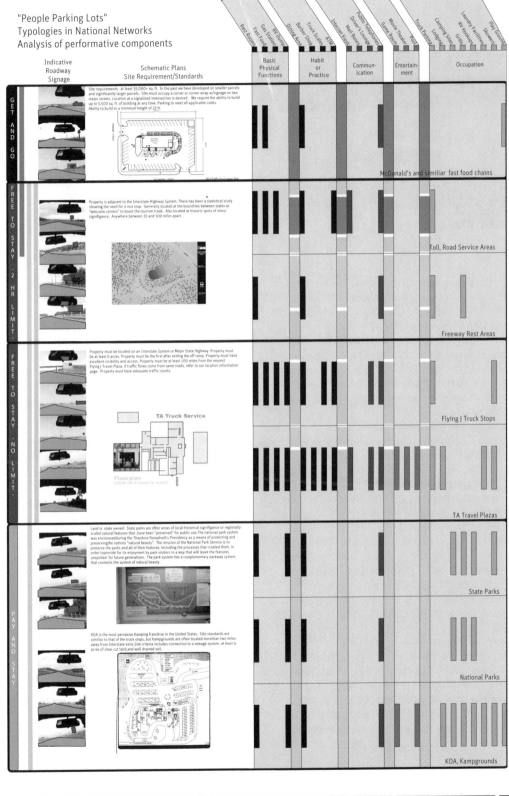

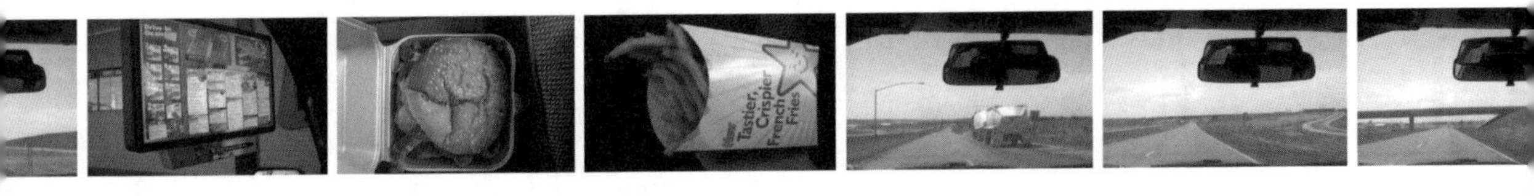

Rest Rooms
Fast Food
Gas Station
RV Dump
Dining Area
Barber Shop
Truck Scales
ATM
Internet Kiosk
Mail Boxes
Driver's Lounge
Public Telephones
Game Room
Movie Theater
Pool
Truck Parking
Lodging
Camping Sites
Grills
RV Hookups
Laundry Facilities
Showers
Play Ground
Indicative Roadway Signage
Schematic Plans
Site Requirement/Standards
Basic Physical Functions
Habit or Practice
Commun-ication
Entertain-ment
Occupation
GET AND GO
Site requirements: at least 35,000+ sq. ft. In the past we have developed on smaller parcels and significantly larger parcels. SIte must occupy a corner or corner wrap w/signage on two major streets. Location at a signalized intersection is desired. We require the ability to build up to 5,500 sq. ft. of building at any time. Parking to meet all applicable codes. Ability to build to a minimum height of 22 ft.
PRIMARY STREET
SECONDARY STREET
McDonald's and similiar fast food chains
FREE TO STAY - 2 HR LIMIT -
Property is adjacent to the Interstate Highway System. There has been a statistical study showing the need for a rest stop. Generally located at the boundries between states as "welcome centers" to boost the tourism trade. Also located at historic spots of minor signifigance. Anywhere between 35 and 100 miles apart.
Toll, Road Service Areas
Freeway Rest Areas
FREE TO STAY - NO LIMIT -
Property must be located on an Interstate System or Major State Highway. Property must be at least 6 acres. Property must be the first after exiting the off ramp. Property must have excellent visibility and access. Property must be at least 100 miles from the nearest Flying J Travel Plaza, if traffic flows come from same roads, refer to our location information page. Property must have adequate traffic counts.
TA Truck Service
Floorplan
(click on a room to view)
Flying J Truck Stops
TA Travel Plazas
PAY AND STAY
Land is state owned. State parks are often areas of local historical signifigance or regionally scaled natural features that ,have been "preserved" for public use.The national park system was envisionedduring the Theodore Rooselvelt's Presidency as a means of protecting and preservingthe nations "natural beauty". The mission of the National Park Service is to preserve the parks and all of their features, including the processes that created them, in order toprovide for its enjoyment by park visitors in a way that will leave the features unspoiled for future generations. The park system has a complementary parkway system that connects the system of natural beauty.
KOA is the most pervasive Kamping franchise in the United States. Site standards are similiar to that of the truck stops, but Kampgrounds are often located morethan two miles away from Interstate exits.Site criteria includes connection to a sewage system, at least 4 acres of clear cut land,and well drained soil.
LEGEND
State Parks
National Parks
KOA, Kampgrounds

Tastier, Crispier French Fries

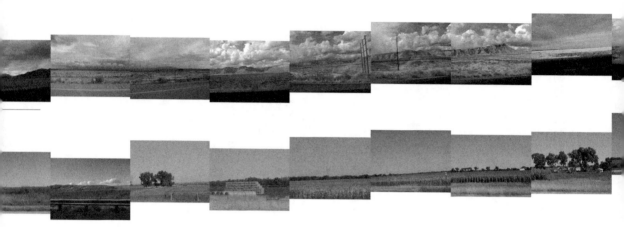

Active Stops are developed locationally following the logic of truck stop plazas. They exist within five miles of an access point on an un-tolled stretch of road. The Active Stop utilizes road-side right-of-way instead of a peripheral zone. Active Stops are designed to be places where drivers can leave their vehicles and be encompassed by a scale that is particular to and negotiable by human proportions without the sea of pavement condition that is often presented by other People Parking Lots.

Active Stops are not discreet entities. They exist in a network and together to define a zone — a stretch of road that would vary between five and fifteen miles. An active zone would be apparent from the inside of a passing vehicle not only because of the presence of signage, but because of the way the signage is rhythmically and systematically placed relative to the road. Their exact locations are determined by conditional parallelisms of supporting infrastructures, such as local roads and electric lines. Active Stops provide a pedestrian link between national and local edges, opening up the development of land that parallels, but does not currently interact with or benefit from, the Interstate Highway system.

Active Stops serve as nodes along a public park space that would run adjacent to the Interstate. This park space is a commercial-free zone on the national edge. The development of the local edge would be dependent upon local decisions, through zoning ordinances and planning organizations. Active Stops provide parking at the national vehicular level, and access to amenities such as public rest rooms on a pedestrian level.

Active Stops would be funded, initially, through grants from the Federal Highway Association's Highway Trust Fund. These grants may take the form of tax and budget incentives that are made available to each state's Department of Transportation. Each Active Stop is programmed with regulated advertising space. Each state would contract with advertisers to generate funds for the maintenance of Active Zones. By exchanging the right to an unhampered view — provided by the Highway Beautiful Act, 1964 — for zones of highly concentrated prime advertising space, funds can be generated to support a secondary type of exchange on national-local edges.

Opening the roadside to pedestrian through-travel is a way to allow for a non-corporate development of the roadside that would not compromise the Interstate's rapid transit goals. The intent of Active Zones and Active Stops is to initiate a blurring of scale throughout the Interstate system. The Interstate may have been built "for the people," but the quality of the local-national interface, or edge, is so strictly defined and controlled as to render it unresponsive and uninviting to drivers.

Lynne Opper is a designer practicing in the backwoods of Massachusetts. About Ways is a culmination of work from her Bachelor of Architecture thesis project, initially developed at Rensselaer Polytechnic Institute's School of Architecture with David Riebe as advisor; Anna Dyson, Michael Oatman and Ken Warriner were reviewers. She is a former RPI BrownsFellow, and conducted much of this research during that time. She has travelled over 13,000 Interstate miles, collecting images, video, and impressions along the way. She enjoys designing and making nice things, as well as observing the byways and highways of the United States from the automobile.

NOTES

1. Acevedo-Riker, Patricia. "Platial Practices," this issue.
2. Ellin, Nan. ed. "Divided We Fall: Gated and Walled Communities in the United States." *The Architecture of Fear*. New York: Princeton Architectural Press, 1997.
3. Russel, James S. "When Suburbs Become Mega-Suburbs." *Architectural Record 08.03*.
4. The Interstate system is *public* in terms of free access by motor vehicles. This excludes tolled portions that were adopted into the system later in its development. Its *public* nature is also relative to motor vehicle ownership. Private industry mediates this meaning of *public* by providing the means to activate the way.
5. McShane, Clay. *Down the Asphalt Path*. New York: Columbia University Press, 1994.
   McShane discusses the development of suburban typology as an evangelical response to urban condition in the United States circa 1870.
6. Steinbeck, John. *Travels with Charley: In Search of America*. New York: Viking Press. 1962.
   Published in 1962, Steinbeck's description of the character of the Interstate system holds quite true today: the food is still "spotless and tasteless; untouched by human hands."
7. Easterling, Keller. *Organization Space*. Cambridge, Mass.: MIT Press, 1999.
   In her chapter "Parallel Networks: Roadsides," Easterling discusses the roadside as an in between zone in terms of jurisdiction and reveals how it has been an active — though easily overlooked — site since the inception of the Interstate System.
8. de Certeau, Michel. *The Practice of Everyday Life*. Berkeley: University of California Press, 1984. Quoted text liberally paraphrased from the chapter, "Making Do: Uses and Tactics."

ACTIVESHELTER

Waiting for the bus is a difficult experience at best. The shelters provided by modern urban bureaucracies are static boxes made from plastic and glass that offer nothing in terms of function or information. Passengers are made to waste time waiting for buses which may or may not arrive; they must stay, and simply hope, with nothing to do.

Activeshelter is a proposal to reexamine the typical public transit shelter by transforming the typical passive box into a dynamic piece of urban infrastructure through the application of emergent technologies. These technologies have a twofold effect: the first is to increase the programmatic and functional utility associated with transit shelters by extending the range of vision available to those who use this infrastructure; the second is to explore the potential impact they may have on the larger urban environment.

73

Waverly
Square

Kenneth Namkung and Nathaniel Skerry

Mechanical Actuator

Tracking Video Camera

Steel Armature

Hinged Translucent
Polycarbonate Surface

Electroactive Polymer Actuators
(Attached to Armature)

Mechanical Connection Between
Armature and Polycarbonate Wings

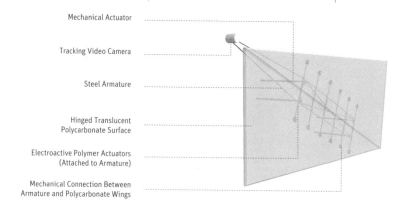

Activewings

Video Camera

Perforated Steel Panel with
Applied Silicone Layer for
Embedded Wiring

LCD Display Screen

Thermal Transfer Seat

Power Generation Surface

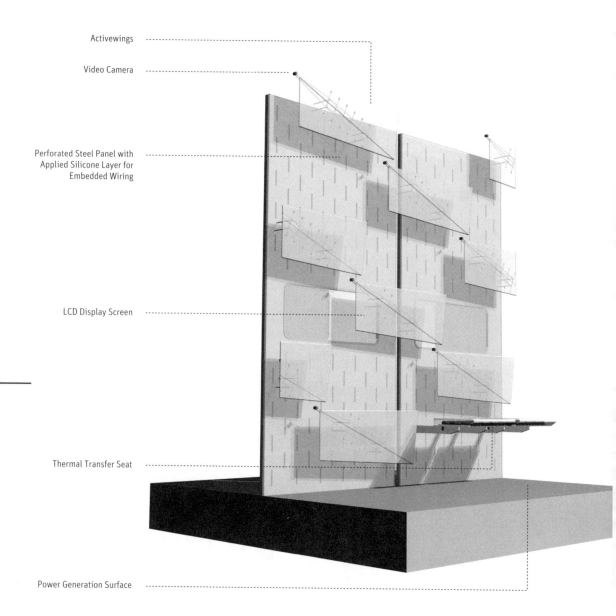

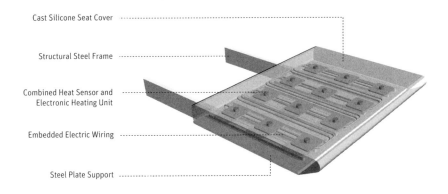

Cast Silicone Seat Cover

Structural Steel Frame

Combined Heat Sensor and
Electronic Heating Unit

Embedded Electric Wiring

Steel Plate Support

Prototype | Pieces

The architectural gestures that define the prototype arise from two primary concerns. The first is the desire to create a prototype that operates on an urban scale by impacting a space beyond the boundaries of the physical object itself. The second is the need to create an architecture with the inherent flexibility to respond to vastly different site conditions. As a result, the primary design gesture eschews the typical repetitive box in favor of a prototype that is the combination of a series of separate and interlinked components, each of which can be modified to respond to a specific locale without imposing a predefined solution on a site.

The first component is an urban canopy; it forms the primary spatial gesture and is over-scaled relative to a typical bus shelter, to create a landmark that responds to the scale of its context. It incorporates lighting elements in the form of a secondary surface layer consisting of an electroluminescent thin film that obviates the need for fixtures. In addition, the canopy incorporates solar films on its upper surface to provide energy for lighting.

The second component is a dynamic wall surface that incorporates additional program and serves as an active display surface that operates at multiple scales and in multiple modes. Its physical construction is a series of layers, beginning with a folded steel plate substrate to which a tactile layer of silicone is applied. The silicone provides a soft layer into which wiring and objects can easily be embedded. The final layer is a series of scales that incorporate mechanical actuation that allow the wall to physically respond to external stimuli. In addition, this wall incorporates display surfaces that are appropriated for multiple uses

The third component is a ground material change from the typical urban hard-scape to a softer, more tactile surface that infiltrates both the adjacent sidewalks and roadways. This serves to inscribe an area of operations that is felt — as a raised pattern beneath shoes — and heard — as cars drive over the surface. It also provides power for the shelter through the use of electroactive polymers.

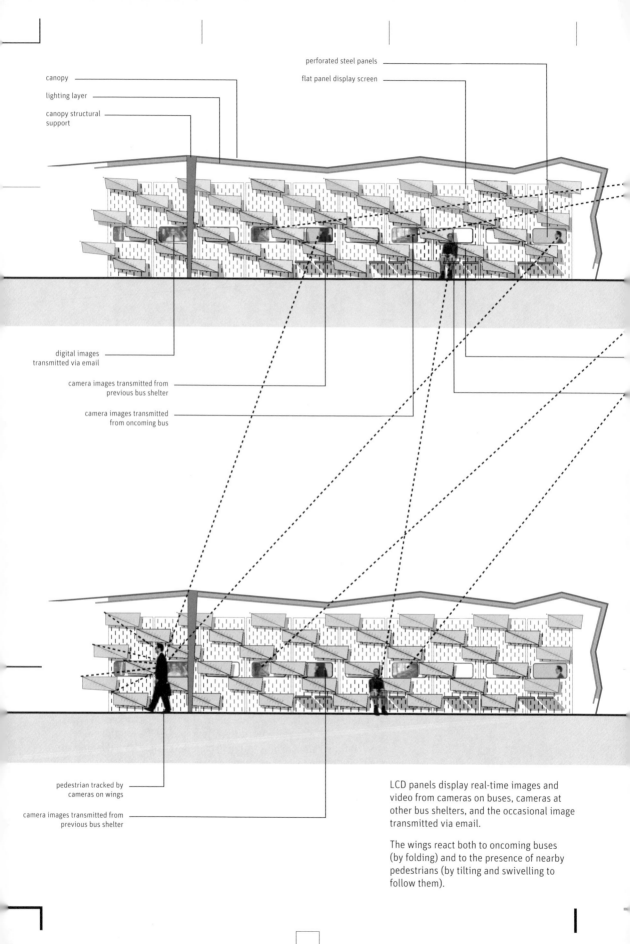

canopy

lighting layer

canopy structural
support

perforated steel panels

flat panel display screen

digital images
transmitted via email

camera images transmitted from
previous bus shelter

camera images transmitted
from oncoming bus

pedestrian tracked by
cameras on wings

camera images transmitted from
previous bus shelter

LCD panels display real-time images and
video from cameras on buses, cameras at
other bus shelters, and the occasional image
transmitted via email.

The wings react both to oncoming buses
(by folding) and to the presence of nearby
pedestrians (by tilting and swivelling to
follow them).

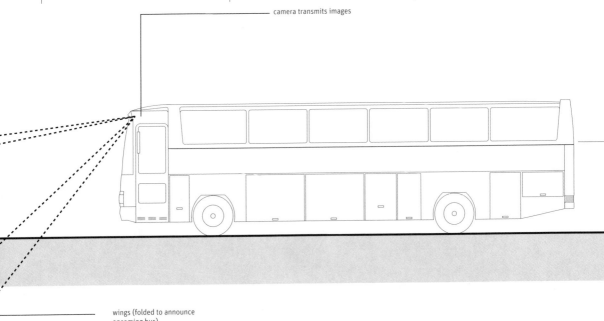

camera transmits images

wings (folded to announce
oncoming bus)

body heat is transmitted from
next bus shelter through seats

Technology | Interactions

The embedded technologies perform a number of distinct tasks. The first
and primary effect is to attempt to increase the amount of contextual
information made available to passersby and riders — in effect, to extend
the range of their vision through electronic means. This is accomplished
through a number of techniques, ranging from ambient modes of
information transmission to more direct methods — such as video
transmission. The methods by which this information is collected and
retransmitted find physical manifestation in the form of an active surface,
which tracks and reacts to changes in the surrounding context.

The scales or wings applied to the wall surface are multifunctional
and dynamic objects. Constructed from a steel armature — actuated
with electroactive polymers — and hinged polycarbonate wings and
incorporating a video camera, the wings embody two types of external
response. The first is to fold uniformly to announce an oncoming bus to
passengers and passersby, making its presence visible even if the bus
itself is not; the wall changes from a flat and passive surface to one with
activity and depth. The second response is to tilt and swivel to track
passing pedestrians using the attached digital video camera. The camera
is then used to wirelessly transmit those images to LCD display panels in
shelters beyond, making activity in one bus shelter visible to passengers in
other shelters.

The display panels are able to receive images from other sources,
such as cameras within buses, cameras attached to wings, and even via
email. This multiplicity of inputs allows for a shifting of readings and the
potential for subversion of intentions by outside influences, requiring
active interpretation on the part of the viewer to understand which images
contain useful information about contexts beyond, and which do not.

Finally, the seat surfaces themselves are capable of this long-
distance information exchange through the transfer of body heat from
one shelter to another. Through the use of heating elements and sensors
embedded into cast silicon seats, the presence of passengers in one shelter
can be made tangible to waiting passengers in another.

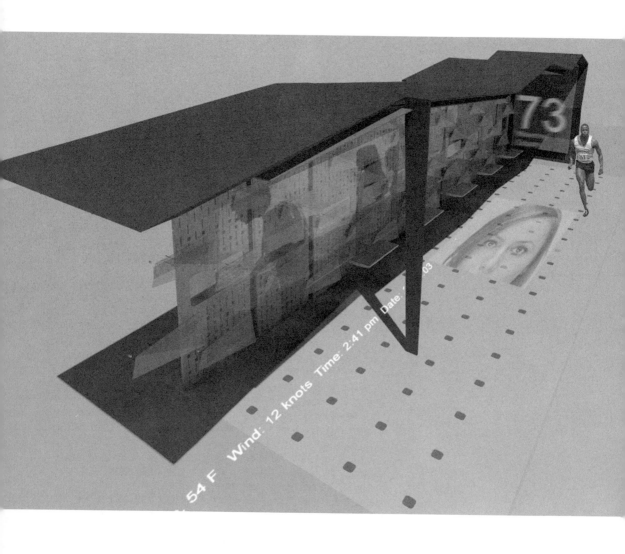

Implications | Overview

Activeshelter serves as a critique of the utilitarianism associated with infrastructural objects. It is hoped that the insertion of emerging technologies into the mundane infrastructures of everyday urban life will allow the proposed architecture to take on a new potential relevance and meaning. Rather than merely suggesting that the introduction of data and image transmission technologies are antithetical or destructive to urbanism and architecture, Activeshelter posits that a more complex relationship exists. Technologies of electronic mediation may serve to intensify the dualistic relationship that exists between urban participants and their context; the give-and-take that already exists can be further deepened. In addition, a certain complexity is added — intimations of surveillance and privacy invasion underscore all the proposed technologies, adding a level of ambivalence to this notion of extended vision.

Nathaniel Skerry holds a Bachelor of Science from Northeastern University and a Master of Architecture from the Massachusetts Institute of Technology. He was involved with the Emergent Material research group at MIT, where he was a project designer for such projects as: Composites and Biocomposites: a natural fiber, a reinforced concrete school building in Venezuela, and a Fabric Skyscraper in New York City. Nathaniel Skerry has professional experience with practices including Office dA, Kallmann, McKinnell and Wood, and Stubbins Associates.

Kenneth Namkung holds a Bachelor of Science in Architecture from the University of Virginia and a Master of Architecture from the Massachusetts Institute of Technology, where he was the recipient of the Marvin E. Goody Prize and the Louis C. Rosenberg Travel Grant. He is currently employed at Rafael Viñoly Architects. He has taught three design studios at the Boston Architectural Center and has participated in design juries at the University of Virginia, MIT, Wentworth Institute of Technology and the Boston Architectural Center.

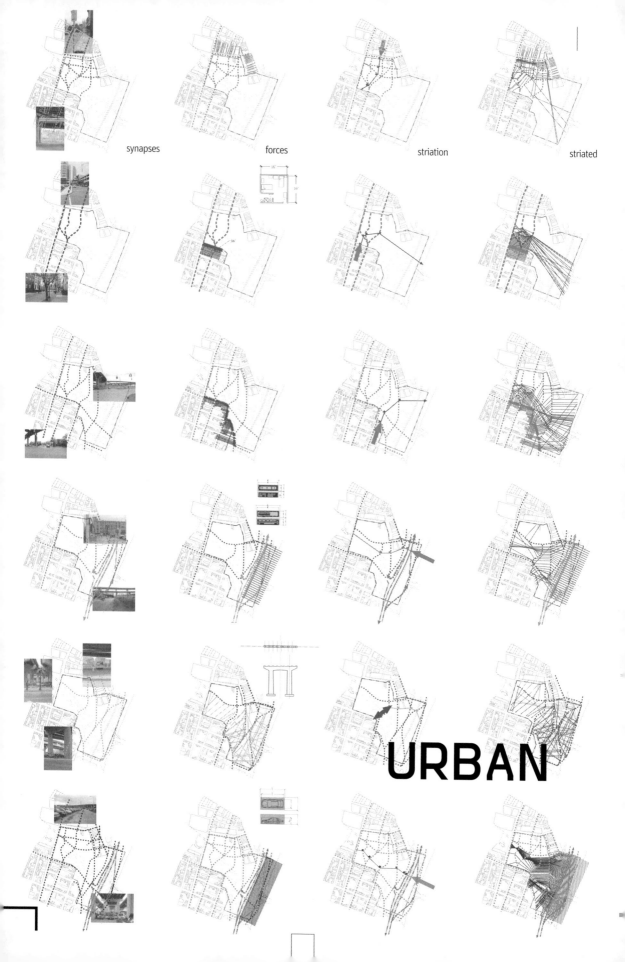

synapses   forces   striation   striated

URBAN

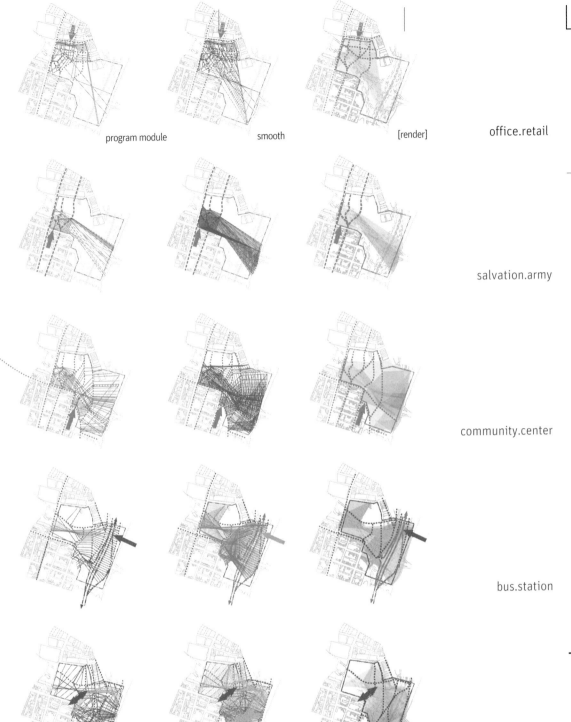

program module   smooth   [render]   office.retail

salvation.army

community.center

bus.station

INFRASTRUCTURE

park

EXPLORING SYSTEMS THAT ENABLE DIVERGENT OCCUPATION OF THE BUILT ENVIRONMENT

DesignLab

parking

Exploring Systems that Enable Divergent Occupation of the Built Environment

Urban infrastructures are flexible systems, allowing for a multiplicity of programs, spatial configurations, architectural typologies, and social structures. They are manifest in live-work relationships, commerce, transportation, public gatherings, recreation, and political activity. Urban infrastructures mitigate disparate conditions while maintaining a restricted and efficient set of parts and pieces. Flexibility is a production of the possibilities created through the repetitious use of a variety of interchangeable parts and pieces, defining limits, narrow or broad to the extents of the system. The system expands and contracts to meet demand within its available limits. Transportation networks, utility lines, demographic dispersions, or social configurations may all be forms of urban infrastructures. We are interested in pushing the limits of urban infrastructures, occupying those systems in subversive ways and creating architecture that explores new possibilities — building upon and stretching a given system — locating itself in its boundaries.

As physical and cultural contexts of existing infrastructural systems shift and change, divergent forms of occupation become possible through alternate programmatic mixes, social organization, and new technology. The established system provides an opportunistic substructure to a new organization, manifesting itself in a palimpsest of new and old systems, a reinterpretation of an existing system, or an addition within a system. These combinations create diverse environments for architectural and urban exploration.

The superimposition of additional infrastructural systems on existing systems allows for layered readings of potential spatial configurations. As systems overlap, integrate and subvert one-another, additional organizational possibilities reveal their ability to be exploited or claimed as tools for design. A revelation may occur as systems and their contextual experience are mapped, analyzed and re-represented — exhibiting their realities that are not obvious in situ. Photography, drawings, diagrams, and models filter and call attention to areas of interest within urban infrastructural systems. Mappings expose latent possibilities within or between systems, divulging scores of contextual readings.

The reuse and subversion of infrastructural systems reflects changing technology, economic shifts, and varying social and political agendas. While many forms of infrastructure may be replaced, flexible systems maintain their identity even as they are transformed. The parts and pieces of a system may be altered in position or function to satisfy an alternate requirement. A system may completely transform through a slow process of rejuvenation that is continually able to meet new needs — all without losing its integral identity.

The modification and adaptation of infrastructural systems in defined locales within a larger structure allows systems to resolve specific needs. The variation permitted by successful infrastructural systems creates a fluid structure, responsive to contextual forces and new insertions. Each variation becomes a result of a specific force — site requirements, programmatic needs, formal arrangements, or social organizations — impressing the character of the catalyst into the infrastructural system. These variations have the potential to blur the line between the infrastructural system and that which it supports.

The thickness created via overlaying and intermeshing of infrastructural systems creates what Stan Allen refers to as field conditions:

A field condition could be any formal or spatial matrix capable of unifying diverse elements while respecting the identity of each. Field configurations are loosely bound aggregates characterized by porosity and local interconnectivity. Overall shape and extent are highly fluid and less important than the internal relationships of parts, which determine the behavior of the field. Field conditions are bottom-up phenomena, defined not by overarching geometrical schemas but by intricate local connections. Interval, repetition, and seriality are key concepts. Form matters, but not so much the forms of things as the forms between things.[1]

Field conditions, as infrastructural systems, are typically horizontal in nature — a thick mesh. The spaces between connections within the horizontal mesh provide opportunities to insert points that may form yet another layer in the ever-fluctuating field condition. The variances between existing conditions and additional systems exhibit the possibility of divergence, the added systems not always remaining within the given constraints of the existing condition, thickening the mesh.

Our typically mundane experiences of these structures belie the complexities of urban infrastructures. Urban infrastructures shape our lives, although we rarely recognize them. The most commonplace and minimal structures are often part of a larger system with functions that we seldom stop to identify. Urban infrastructures form the backdrop to productive systems. They are ripe for exploration.

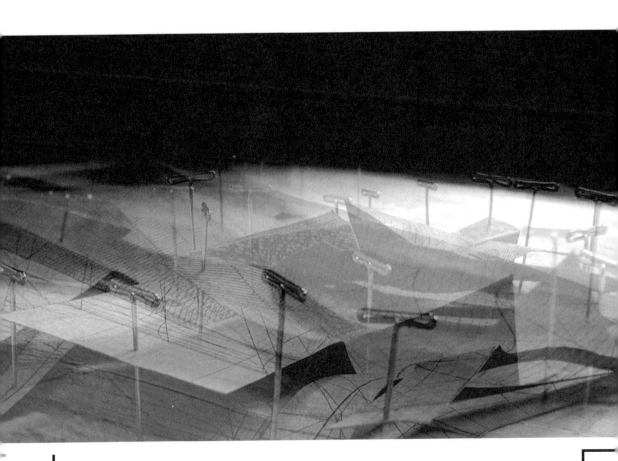

VORHIZOMEID: NODES OF COMMUNITY SERVICES CONNECTING ALBANY, NY

Andrew Watkins

The fragmented condition of the twenty-first century city has left voids of opportunity that anticipate occupation. Fragmentation from the insertion of transportation infrastructure has created adjacent residual voids within its surrounding urban fabric. The city has been pulled away from its association with the human by the insertion of infrastructure into the spaces of which humans occupy. The disparate scales surrounding these voids leave them with no membership, no belonging to their bordering conditions. The resultant condition is fertile for exploration.

Ignasi de Solà-Morales Rubio has coined the term *terrain vague* to describe voids in relation to the city, an example being the residual voids of transportation infrastructure as it slices through urban fabric. Solà-Morales' description of the terrain vague positions these spaces not as negative spaces that must be renewed but as opportunistic spaces for a different type of urban architecture. Solà-Morales describes this in his essay *Terrain Vague.*

> When architecture and urban design project their desire onto a vacant space, a terrain vague, they seem incapable of doing anything other than introducing violent transformations, changing estrangement into citizenship, and striving at all costs to dissolve the uncontaminated magic of the obsolete in the realism of efficacy. To employ a terminology current in the aesthetics underlying Gilles Deleuze's thinking, architecture is forever on the side of forms, of the distant, of the optical and the figurative, while the divided individual of the contemporary city looks for forces instead of forms, for the incorporated instead of the distant, for the haptic instead of the optic, the rhizomatic instead of the figurative.[2]

The contention is to reposition terrain vague into the urban fabric, recreating a continuum of the urban system while attempting to detract neither from the scale of the infrastructural system, nor that of the human body. Terrain vague must be approached in a different manner than that of the traditional urban city. Establishing continuity through terrain vague should be done by measure of the forces, flows, and rhythms of the space. Albany, New York contains an expectant void close to its effective circuits of the city. I-787 connects the center of the city, the capitol complex, with I-87, the major north-south freeway passing by Albany from New York City. As I-787 travels along the Hudson River it interchanges with Routes 9 and 20, allowing access to the capitol complex. This access cuts through the city, leaving a void that runs from the capitol complex down to the river and separating the main business district from a dense mixed-use area to the south.

The intention is to occupy this void with multiplicity of programmatic elements that respond to the forces of the surrounding neighborhoods. The ability of the program to mediate these forces allows it to connect the disparate systems of the city, meshing them into a smooth, cohesive system. The program will consist of a Community Center, Salvation Army Center, park and recreational spaces, regional bus station, small stores and offices, and parking garages. Each element responds to the needs of the surrounding communities — their social, economic, and infrastructural disabilities that have forced them apart around the void of the site.

synapses

the synapse is a space of connection between two effective circuits. in neuroscience it is the space between two neuron cells that allows for the passage of information without altering the spatial characteristics of the space between cells. in Albany, the synapse is a space of connection that occupies the void without changing the void's smoothness

forces

forces have a direction from the site context combined with a spacing influenced by program either as a continuation of a site condition or as an introduction of a new program

striation

the forces are organized according to the layout of the synapses. when a force comes in contact with a synapse, it shifts direction perpendicular to the synapse - similar to shifts created in street grids as one street shifts, its crosstrees follow perpendicularly

striating

the organization of forces by the synapse become varied due to the curvature of its path. forces cross one another, diverge and converge

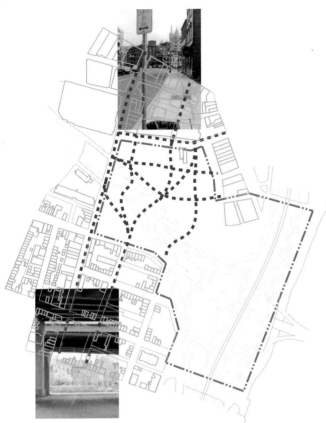

Office.retail_synapses

program module

the forces, which inscribe an organization of a program type in relation to the site become more defined by a second dimension which completes the module of a programmatic type.

smooth

the ensuing organizational system becomes so striated that its reading is lost and results in a smooth system. the smooth system, since its generation, provides horizontal organization. while verticality is implied by areas that are less clear about their striation, thereby more clear about their smoothness, no specific rule is given for the vertical manipulation of and by this system. the areas that become of most interest are those where the greatest densification coincides with the synapses that are generating their organization.

[render]

render of densities allows a clearer reading of horizontal organization. this graphic representation can serve as a simple clue towards placements of program but should not be removed from its relationship to the striations and their smoothing.

Community center_striated

ADDRESSING THE ISSUES OF TRANSPORTATION— DEFINED LIFE PATTERNS OF SUBURBAN SPRAWL

Jeremy Munn

Suburban sprawl has liberated architecture from the limits of urban context and human scale. With the high speed of the automobile, the architecture designed for the timing of the pedestrian scale has been replaced with signage and wider roads. No longer are environments being designed for the scale, pace, pattern and bounds of the human scale.[3]

With the perception of time drastically changing the built environment, the scale of the pedestrian is lost. Now that the scale of the automobile has replaced the human scale in defining life patterns, sprawl, traffic congestion, pollution and isolation exist.

For the transportation-defined life-pattern of today's suburbanites, a new transportation system can mediate between the relationship of time and scale of the pedestrian and the automobile as well as alleviate points of pressure.
Transportation infrastructure can act as an active architectural participant to define a sense of center in suburbia.
A sense of experiential space can be defined by creating a circuit of directions to harness infrastructural forces.

Central Islip, NY, located about one hour east of Manhattan in Suffolk County, presents itself as a prime example of suburban sprawl. With the town's growth generated around the use of the automobile, a lack of hierarchy exists. With no clearly defined center, and physical fragmentation defining the placement of public buildings, the town has been liberated from the limits of urban context and human scale. The challenge exists to be able to organize the existing sprawl by introducing a new transportation system.

An intermodal train station and a series of substations could be the answer to the organization of existing sprawl. By connecting the intermodal train station to the existing high speed Long Island Rail Road network, and creating substations at key points within the existing fabric, urban context and the human scale can be re-introduced.

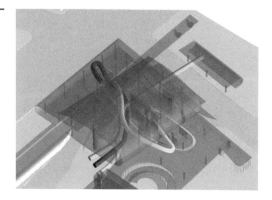
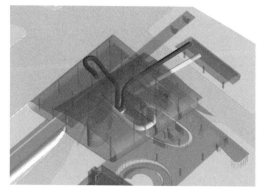

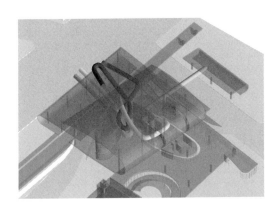 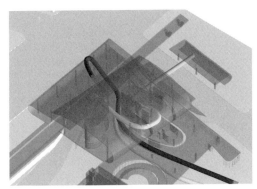

Design-Lab is an interdisciplinary collaborative actively pursuing research and practice in design — focusing on architecture, graphic design and photography. Founded in 2002 by Andrew Watkins and Jeremy Munn, Design-Lab is committed to the exploration of design processes valuing the dialogue between disciplines of design for comprehensive solutions to traditional and non-traditional problems. Design-Lab is interested in connections within and to the field of design that promote and foster theoretical dialogues with practical applications.

Jeremy Munn received a Bachelor of Architecture degree, cum laude from Syracuse University in 2002 where he received the Alpha Rho Chi Medal for Leadership, Merit and Service. His thesis, addressing the issues of the transportation defined life patterns of suburban sprawl, explored perceptions of time and its relationship to human scale. Terrance Goode, Susan Henderson, and Scott Ruff were thesis committee members for this project.

Professional office experience includes positions with JRS Architect of Mineola, NY, and Childs Bertman Tseckares of Boston, MA. Jeremy is also a founding member of Design-Lab. Teaching experience includes instructing a studio at The Boston Architectural Center, a lecturer and guest critic at the New York Institute of Technology, Central Islip, and a guest critic at Northeastern University.

Andrew Watkins received a bachelor of architecture degree, magna cum laude from Syracuse University in 2002 where he received the Luther Gifford Prize in Architecture for Highest Rank in Scholarship. After graduating he won the Mark and Pearl Clements Internship Award and spent the summer working with Andrea Ponsi Architetto in Florence, Italy. His thesis, *vorhizomeid*, was presented for SuperJury and received a citation for design excellence. Bruce Coleman, Mark Linder and Dan Hisel were thesis committee members for this project.

Professional office experience includes positions with Bohlin Cywinski Jackson, Andrea Ponsi Architetto, Childs Bertman Tseckares, and currently in a research fellowship with Moshe Safdie and Associates entitled *Tall Buildings in the City*. Andrew is also a founding member of Design-Lab. Teaching experience includes instructing drawing with the Environmental Design and Interiors program in Florence Italy, instructing studios at The Boston Architectural Center, and as a guest critic at Northeastern University.

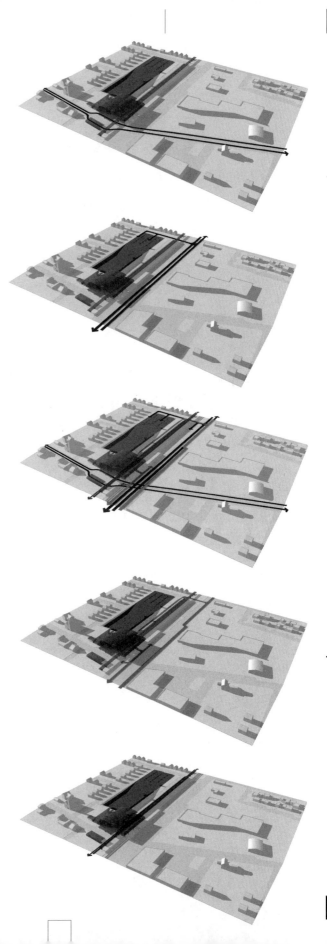

NOTES
1. Stan Allen. *Field Conditions. Points + Lines: Diagrams and Projects for the City.* New York: Princeton Architectural Press. 1999.
2. Solà-Morales Rubio, Ignasi de. "Terrain Vague." *Anyplace.* Cynthia Davidson, ed. Cambridge, Mass: MIT Press, 1995.
3. Peter Calthorpe. *The Next American Metropolis: Ecology, Communities and the American Dream.* New York: Princeton Architectural Press, 1993.

A DANCE ABOUT EMPTINESS

Seth Cluett

As a dancer moves, they carve their way through space; each carefully made motion hewn through both space and time. The motions have a residue, an afterimage in the mind of the on-looker. The space moved through and the space to come is in equilibrium with the body. The term *ma* from Japanese *Noh* theatre helps describe this. In the Japanese language, *ma* can refer to both space and time. In architecture, *ma* means space, for a musician *ma* means time. The movement happens as music moves through time in the space of architecture: architecture is a frozen dance.

As the pencil moves, lines and gestures carve their way through space; each carefully made line in two dimensions giving way to the next, cutting through what will be three-dimensional shape in the finished building. There is a concept in *Noh* about creating a positive or charged empty space. The silence becomes as strong as the sound; power is given to the void. Emptiness gains active potential. The walls of the room become sound, the air in the room is the charged silence of anticipation, and all action with in the space becomes the dance.

To build is to put a skin around emptiness. This skin, the solids of walls, ceilings, and floors define the verbs of space perception: walking, running, and navigating. By defining the potential of the volume of air within, the skin gives the potential for movement, for action. The empty space, the air quality, sound, light, and smell then become in part responsible for adjectives: comfortable, happy, and antsy. The empty space, the *stuff* of the empty space, gives rise to the way action is felt within the space.

Architects build and shape the sets for the dance of the occupants. In this way, the building is the architect's choreography frozen in both time and space. When you walk through the built environment as well as nature, you are carving your way through a sea of air, your movements. . . charged with potential.

"There is vacuity in things," asserts Lucretius in his De Rarum Natura, a space in which solid bodies can move. It is this empty space that affords motion by providing a substance against which we can place solid bodies. The building itself is at equilibrium between the space moved through and the space to come.

Seth Cluett is an installation artist and educator living and working in Troy, NY. His research focuses on the effect of sound and light wave propagation on space perception and cognition. His work has been exhibited and performed at the ICMC in Habana, Cuba and the Acoustical Society of America; the ICA, Mobius Artist Space, MassArt/nonpod in Boston; Diapason and Engine 27 Galleries, The Knitting Factory, and ABCnoRio in New York; Deep Listening Space in Kingston; and Betty Rymer Gallery at the Art Institute of Chicago, Heaven, Artemisia Galleries and Deadtech in Chicago, amongst others. Seth's work is documented on *Errant Bodies Press*, *Kissy*, *Crank Satori*, and *Wavelet* records, as well as an upcoming releases on *Sedimental* and *BoxMedia*.

http://www.onelonelypixel.org

CONTINUITY AND DISCONTINUITY IN THE PHYSICAL AND VIRTUAL SPACE

Yehuda Greenfield

The central problem occupying Adorno's thought can be summarized in the term Culture Industry which refers to a host of cultural products manufactured by the entertainment sphere of mass culture, amusement devices and leisure activities. According to Adorno, the culture industry flatters its consumers; it pretends to be attuned to their needs, cater to their wishes and fulfill their dreams. In reality this industry "exploits its assumed consideration and attentiveness toward the masses to replicate, consolidate and strengthen their mentality, which it perceives to be an unchangeable given fact."

The reality is a much more severe phenomenon related to physical space than either Adorno or Bourdieu anticipated. The space of Late Capitalism, its possibilities, its virtuality and its innumerable images consist of a deceitful and glowing spectrum of contradicting spaces existing simultaneously within and without our consciousness. This space which, in the modernistic era of continuity was presumed to be streamed-lined, simple and effective, is not evidently so anymore. Its morphology has changed into inconsistent shapes and broken lines which show it now to be a considerably less cohesive — and much more unpredictable — system.

Popular culture of consumption, vis-à-vis the virtual media, profoundly affects the physical spaces we inhabit. As such, the consequences of the relationship between our perception of reality, our grasp of physical space, and the increasing burden of consciousness that we experience require examination at the beginning of the 21st century.

Phenomenon No. 1:
Replication of Physical Space

The discovery of the steam locomotive and the establishment of railroads in the mid-nineteenth century succeeded, maybe more than anything else, in defining the conceptual structure of early modern thought. Remarkably efficient movement from point A to point B was linked to the presumption that we move in a direction of constant progress. The notion of modernity raised the concept of continuity to the level of a worldview: direct movement between goals, where point B is always a more advanced state than A.

The United States can serve as a case study regarding the establishment of physical space in accord with the underlying presumptions of modernity. By observing a society which has committed itself by its constitution to modern presumptions, we can examine how these abstract ideas emerge and solidify as fundamental hypotheses for organizing physical space. In the United States, as elsewhere in the capitalistic world,

the large cities are production centers generating the most influential seminal processes of political, economic and industrial initiatives. In such urban centers as New York, Chicago, Los Angeles, these processes proceed in the paradigmatic tradition of modernity, driven by the energy of their forefathers and leaders, constituting the great engine which propels the American reality forward.

In parallel with the development of powers and dimensions of the center points of modernity, came along a myth of vectors which constitute the mechanism linking point A to point B — the highways and railroads designed to transport millions of people from one large city to another. This system of points and vectors creates the modernistic network of goals and movement toward them. This network, corresponding to the notion of continuity, however, does not comprise the complete or comprehensive mapping of the populated spaces of the United States. Strung out along the huge American highway system are hundreds of thousands of small towns, all of which seem to be fashioned after the same design: central road, gas station, motels, local church, stores and residential dwellings. It appears that these towns sprouting along the main highway do not fit into the scheme of continuity. They are to be found neither at A nor B, at neither an origin nor an objective, but merely an accident — at best a corridor, a means to

an end, transitional. We can perceive, then, behind the network of progress characterized by points and directions, a sub-network of spaces that are not part of the scheme of continuity, but rather constitute an intermediate space that includes all these Anytowns.

This phenomenon takes on an additional spatial expression of the greatest importance: unlike the large cities — which aspire to produce their own specific economic and cultural brand names, be it Wall Street or Soho in New York, The National Gallery of Art in Washington DC, Hollywood or Beverly Hills in L.A., General Electric or Sears in Chicago, Harvard University near Boston, The Space Center in Houston, etc. — these intermediary spaces, representatives of a sub-network increasingly resemble one another. Almost all share the same fundamental plan, differing only in minor details of local geography. Similarly, the huge commercial centers and malls also remain outside the network of continuity. Not only are these small intermediaries devoid of significant identity, but their sole source of comprehension and meaning derives from the main focal points of production at the end of the highway, leaving them with a system of significance entirely borrowed from others. One can presume the consequences for the spatial self image of these towns is substantial. Could there exist a link between the replicate-like resemblance

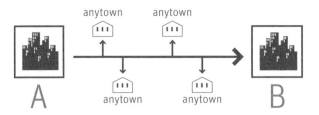

anytown   anytown

A   anytown   anytown   B

among those spaces and the fact of their being — in some sense — irrelevant?

The link between the two phenomena does not occur by chance. The resemblance between those intermediary spaces is to a large extent the spatial expression of their ejection from the network of modernistic goals and their relegation to the sub-network of discontinuity.

Phenomenon No. 2:
Replication of Virtual Space[1]

It is impossible not to recognize the power of television as one of the most popular instruments promulgating fantasized images of reality. Many of our notions about quality of life, success, and happiness derive from the virtual-television medium. Pierre Bourdieu claims that television has surreptitiously become a tool for symbolic oppression, applying "violence inflicted by means of the consent implied by the silence of those who fall victim to it — and frequently of those perpetrating it, with neither aware of being perpetrator or victim." Television's effectiveness, according to Bourdieu, is achieved through continuous and powerful censorship hidden from the eye, preventing the users from realizing the true nature of reported events. The decision what to broadcast and what to ignore, says Bourdieu, determines the very nature of television, and falls into two basic categories.

The first is the category of negation. The network is inclined not to report information that may damage its own very objective: to increase revenues. Reports on the corruption of its own managers, for instance, or the failures of its major financial resources will not be aired.

Second is the category of affirmation. Even though the networks may trumpet their commitment to utterly objective reporting, it is clear that their primary concern is to survive economically and to make a profit. Therefore ratings emerge as the preeminent force determining all considerations, especially in the world of globalism and capitalism in which commercial television is one of the most immediately recognizable elements. The familiar craving for the extraordinary is exploited by television and vulgarized into the search for the sensational. The daily news broadcast has to present on a mundane, daily schedule something

which transcends the mundane; this is not easy, but is, rather, a terrible constraint the pursuit of the scoop. It is clear that the laws of profitability and success in the ratings game completely change the television commodity. This commodity, whether a news program or interview, takes on new characteristics which Bourdieu calls the circular flow of information. "Before my eyes appears the idea that the journalistic product is far more homogeneous than we think. The seeming differences obscure a deep underlying similarity among them, related especially to the constraints imposed on them by their sources. I have noticed that competition between newspapers subjected to the same constrains, to the same polls and the same advertisers, creates homogeneity. Compare the front pages of the daily newspapers in France once in a fortnight — the headlines are more or less identical." The nightly news, guest interviews and prime-time shows, as they pass through the ratings grinder, end up being some sort of a product, all similar, abiding by the same rules imposed by competition.

It appears that Bourdieu's description depicts the process by which global information networks reduce their colossal potential for knowledge distribution into superficial homogeneous units of trivialities, intended to serve only the *Lord of Ratings* and becoming one of the most powerful instruments repressing reality.

The wish to create a streamlined continuity of the money making process stimulates television to invent optimal ways of satisfying popular demand. Ironically, this great symbol of modernity, efficiency, and democratization, the supposedly open line of free information flowing to all parts of the world, finds itself again in a different field creating stamped-out, replicated copies of virtual spaces, devoid of internal purpose and meaning except for their function as service stations on the money pumping highway to huge corporate profits. The doses of television programs we absorb in the form of prime-time shows or the nightly news are the stock products of the ratings enterprise, a product specializing in replication of reality derived again from the special demands of the logic of competition. Once again we encounter this paradigmatic model of a continuity driving forward, breaking down into replicated end variants of space.

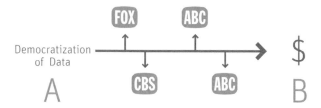

The Connection

We can now compare the two phenomena. The Anytowns," lacking independent self-definition, all acquire a similar countenance, as if space itself has undergone many replications; Anytowns are the intermediate components in the continuous system of distribution — interstates, suburban developments, chain stores — extant between major cities.

In parallel, there exists a more abstract model, likewise linear in direction. The homogeneity of televised media — regardless of program type — results from common intentions and methods within the television industry. The goal is usually to make a profit, but this must happen virtually, via advertising support and popularity ratings. This equation, ratings = profits continuously supplies moulds for the mass replication of the television product.

The basic relationship between these two phenomena becomes clear in terms of a principle Bourdieu calls the Zhdanov Effect, derived from research conducted by a literary critic named Sapiro, who studied the behavior of French writers during the Nazi occupation in France. He came to the conclusion that collaboration with the Nazi regime was mostly depended on what he defined as their symbolic capital, namely the esteem they hold in the eyes of their colleagues. The more respect and appreciation they have enjoyed in the literary community, the less they were inclined to collaborate. In contrast, the more a writer allowed external circumstances and commercial concerns to influence his literary praxis thus earning the contempt of his colleagues, the greater the likelihood of becoming a collaborator.

The term symbolic capital deserves elaboration. It seems that people who are highly regarded by their peers enjoy a position of moral and professional authority. However, their unique symbolic capital pertains not to material assets but to sources of identity, energy and creativity. Those with symbolic capital are disciplined and inspired by an inner system of principles and directions, enabling them to conduct his or her life from within, rather than from the outside. Symbolic capital, then, relates to the internal reservoir of intellectual and moral forces from which the individual draws his or her capacity to contend with difficulties, to perform moral and esthetical judgments, to embrace new horizons, to harbor new ideas and to embark on new initiatives.

This idea of symbolic capital can be applied to our subject as well. We can contrast the metropolis, in which great reality-defining political, economic and cultural processes take place, rich in symbolic capital, with inter-urban towns left without it. When a space, physical or virtual, lacks this independent generative ability, which might have enabled it to become a goal and not merely a means, it tends to acquire an arbitrary content. It begins to lose its particularity, and its external features begin to fade into the flat existence of endlessly replicated anonymity. In virtual space symbolic capital is no less relevant. Networks, which for reasons of profit are dependent on ratings, demonstrate preferences that are not conducive to high professional journalistic standards. By yielding to capitalistic pressures they injure their propensity to accumulate symbolic capital. The abandonment of symbolic capital leaves the networks with the necessity — and the opportunity — to endow their products with alternative qualifications, more relevant to money-making aims, and repeat the empty yet efficient formula endlessly.

The similarity between the two phenomena calls for attention: what happens when actual physical spaces along the continuity line of transportation, and virtual spaces along the continuity line of the capitalistic endeavor lose their intrinsic significance and become means rather than ends, devoid of symbolic capital of their own? What fills the vacuum?

Therein lies the central argument of this paper: these two phenomena of replicated physical space and replicated virtual space nourish one another, forming a sort of closed symbiotic circle within a universe lacking its own symbolic capital. This symbiotic circle comprises two systems of relationships. The first system works as follows:

> 1. The replicated physical space influences the replicated virtual space.

Innumerable studies indicate that in the United States, the extent of television viewing among various sociological sectors is striking.[2] It is not surprising, then, that small-town residents are usually considered to be heavy consumers of TV. One can presume that physical spaces poor in existential significance will attempt to draw significance from other sources.

It is very likely that increased television consumption, with its rich panoply of sparkling and enticing images dancing across the screen, fulfils exactly this purpose. Virtual reality extends far beyond mere reality; it represents a kind of hyper-reality. Sacredness and authority are imparted on its contents via its hyper-visibility. TV's incomparable visibility is the fulfillment of the charismatic power which transforms broadcasted material into magic and imparts its shows and stars with the embodiment of the "source of existence," the Logos.[3] Because the internal significance possessed by physically replicated spaces remains in doubt, inhabitants of such spaces grasp at the key images, which dominate the realm of replication itself — that is to say, celebrities and heroes of artificial reality. Those very figures, whom television redeemed from anonymity and lent meaning to their lives by turning them into stars — in Berkeley's words, "to be is to be seen" — now become the redeemers of the inhabitants of replicated space. The medium of television determines their reality by imparting on them its own virtual conception of life. Through television they discover what happiness is, what love is, what expectations they should develop and to what ends they should aspire. Through the unique situation of the physical, the virtual system has gained unimagined power.

2.The replicated virtual space influences the replicated physical space.

"The power of the image broadcast over and over, like the collapse of the Twin Towers on September 11, is its ability to achieve a new some firm grounding within actual reality. The actual that penetrates into our lives has the status of mere appearance...precisely because it is actual, that is to say, because of its traumatic and exaggerated character we are unable to assimilate it into our reality. Therefore we have no choice but to regard it as a nightmarish vision. That is how we experienced the riveting picture of the collapsing towers: an image repeated over and over, perceived by the eye, a parallel *effect* which is substituted for the thing itself."[5]

The characteristics of the late capitalist space, semi-virtual and often replicated, enable television to be a powerful tool for mediation between our consciousness and reality. This tool is strengthened considerably when aided by concrete physical spaces, which mediate between television reality and the physical spaces of doubtful internal significance. These spaces, constructed to enhance consumption in the hope of acquiring symbolic capital, include malls, Power centers and motels. Like the replicated spaces themselves, malls and motels are externally identical. They are generally located in intermediary zones: not within the city itself, but on its outskirts. Like the Anytowns, malls are replicates of the same nature — consumer-oriented, anonymous and serving a mediating function. To a large degree they embody a virtual ideology in the physical space. They serve as interlocutors between our consciousness within physical space and television-virtual reality. In the mall, physical space meets the world of images, brand names, fashion, logos, consumerism and cinema, all familiar to us from our television screen. The promised land of commodity suddenly comes to life, materialized in flesh and blood products, which are magically transported from the television screen into the mall.

Thus we complete the nutritive cycle. Inhabitants of the replicated spaces consume images from virtual reality, provided by the television, the secret of whose power lies in its ability to mediate between us and the world of replicated, virtual space. Thus, in a cyclical fashion, television users derive their existence from the images that dance across the screen; the television in turn derives its power from its ability to present and filter external reality.

Here several related questions can be asked: Is this cycle unchangeable? Does this nutritive cycle oblige the continuous replication of space? Is there a way — or a need — to consider when a physical space ceases to be a copy of its predecessors and acquires individuality? Do we need to seek a new version of television culture, the product of which is not a single program dictated by ratings? In order to answer these questions we need to consider the consequences of the replicated product. What impact it has on us our conception of the world and our understanding of reality?

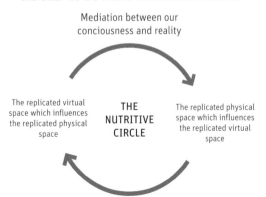

Mediation between our conciousness and reality

The replicated virtual space which influences the replicated physical space

THE NUTRITIVE CIRCLE

The replicated physical space which influences the replicated virtual space

The "authority" of Television

Approach to the Problem

The criticism of the virtual, replicated territories does not represent merely a protest against the conduct of the televised, but rather an effort to identify a pattern of conduct which sustains a closed cycle of replication.

Bourdieu does not merely criticize the pattern of conduct of the media. He tries to show us the influence of virtual reality on our understanding of physical reality. That is to say, we are not dealing with a warning against a closed circle of replicative nourishment, but rather we have a substantial problem, one difficult expression of which can be found in televised realities, "the feeling is that the world, as television represents it, does not offer ordinary mortals any anchoring point." The closed cycle of replicate spaces furnishing each other with fantasized existential identity enhances and magnifies our feeling of alienation, dread and lack of connectedness. In the same way, the product of replicated physical space — the same identical towns everywhere — represents the fragmented remains of space which fall through the holes in the modernistic network of Continuity. The journalistic product has a parallel in the virtual reality. The patterns within the nutritive circle still correspond well with each other, producing the very same effect from one replication to the other and from one Discontinuity to the other.

The perils of Continuity, as expressed in this article, are not mentioned without certain bewilderment. If we speak in terms of a solution or approach to the problem, we must invest additional energy. Bourdieu sketches in his imagination a sort of journalistic utopia: "We can imagine agreements among newspapers to neutralize some of the influences of competition . . . I am dabbling here in veritable utopia, and I know it well . . ." Bourdieu seeks to undermine the Zhdanov Effect by investing the journalistic system with symbolic capital which would enable it to focus on goals of substance instead of compromising their values in pursuit of the scoop.

This terminology can also be adapted to physical space. The problem, as originally formulated, concerned the lack of significance of discontinuous physical spaces in the Continuity network, resulting in these spaces replicating themselves endlessly. They find their redemption in consumption of replicated images, repeated in replicated virtual spaces, taking the form of television programs scattered along the persistently continuous line to profit.

One can try to examine ways to invest certain intermediate spaces with symbolic capital. Perhaps this can be achieved through the concept of twin cities, in which relationships are established between intermediate towns suffering from low self-esteem and large cities that have many resources of symbolic capital to offer. A relationship based on shared educational projects, on student exchanges and on mutual creative investment might allow replicate towns beset by a troubled self-image to define their place on the map, by way of the imprimatur derived from adopting the goal disposition and developing an appetite for authentic expressions of solid existence. In addition, one can regard symbolic capital as one regards myth. The city of Edinburgh, for instance, is a smallish city far from the center of Europe. Yet it has managed to create for itself a unique source of symbolic capital by establishing a world renowned annual arts and music festival, drawing hundreds of thousands of visitors — symbolic capital developers. Another example, in the realm of architecture, is the case of the city of Bilbao. Formerly an obscure border town in the Basque region of northern Spain, Bilbao acquired significant prestige by virtue of Frank Ghery's art museum built there. The museum has become an immediate source of myth, creating symbolic capital. One can imagine many ways of approaching the challenge of imparting symbolic capital to a particular space, transforming it from a means alone to an end, a goal.

NOTES

1. Bourdieu, Pierre. *On Television*. Tel Aviv: Babel, 1996.
2. Csikszentmihalyi, M. & Kubey R. "Television Addiction Is No Mere Metaphor". *Scientific American*, February 2002
3. In my opinion, this is the origin of the ability of certain live television programs to bring about reconciliation, right during the broadcast, between father and son who haven't spoken in fifteen years or between feuding couples locked in perpetual conflict. The status of visibility together with the fact of live broadcast impart to the event the power of truth and stamp it with the stamp of this really happened, and right now, in front of millions of viewers, my life took a decisive turn.

Yehuda Greenfield was born in 1976 in New York City, and in 1981 immigrated with his family to Israel. Currently in his fifth year in the Faculty of Architecture at the Technion-Israel Institute of Technology in Haifa, he is busy with his final term project entitled *The Border in Jerusalem—Architecture and Politics.* He has been working for about a year in an architectural firm in Jerusalem.

Yehuda serves as an emissary of the Jewish agency to Jewish communities over the world, giving seminars to students dealing with issues such as tolerance, mutual understanding and co-existence in the Middle East. He likes to read, design lamps and scuba-dive.

306090 06 was made possible by the generous support of
School of Architecture, Rensselaer Polytechnic Institute

For their generous contributions,
306090 wishes to thank:

Richard H. Driehaus Foundation
The Graham Foundation for Advanced Studies in the Fine Arts
Robbin Dripps and Lucia Phiney

and

The School of Architecture, Princeton University
Bakery Group
The Hillier Group
The Michael Sorkin Studio

M. Christine Boyer
David and Jessica Brace
Beatriz Colomina
Claire Flom
Leslie and Peter Flom
Jason and Wendy Flom
David L. Hays
Allen and Ruth Kramer
Margot Krasojevic
Anne R. Kreeger
Nancy Laing
Kevin Lippert
Sadashiv Mallya
Marcin Padlewski and Anissa Szeto
Lora and Tom Sandberg
Richard Solomon
André Soluri
Cara Soh

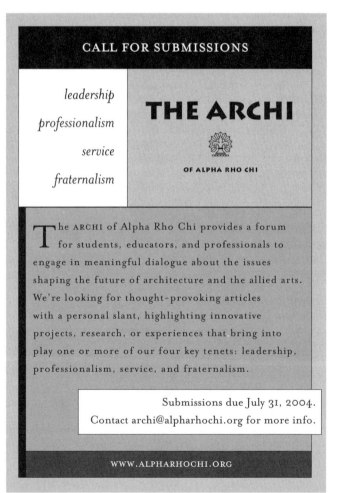

Patricia Acevedo-Riker holds a Bachelor of Science in Environmental Design from the Universidad de Puerto Rico and a Master of Architecture from Rensselaer Polytechnic Institute. She lives and works in Pensacola, Florida as an architecture intern and graphic designer.

Martha Merzig holds a Bachelor of Architecture and a Bachelor of Science in Building Science from Rensselaer Polytechnic Institute, where she was awarded the Ricketts Prize in 2002. Currently, Martha works as an architecture intern at M1/DTW in Detroit.

John Riker holds a Bachelor of Architecture and a Bachelor of Science in Building Science from Rensselaer Polytechnic Institute. He traveled extensively in Vietnam as a Browns Fellow studying and mapping post-colonial urban morphology. Currently, John is pursuing a career in military aviation.

Jeremi Sudol holds a Bachelor of Science in Computer Science and Psychology from Rensselaer Polytechnic Institute and is completing a Master of Science in Computer Science at New York University. He currently works at the Center for Advanced Technology at NYU.

Emily Abruzzo holds a Bachelor of Arts in Architecture from Columbia University and a Master of Architecture from Princeton University. Through her thesis work and her work with AtopiaUK, her research and design have focused on the institutional and ecological factors surrounding the concept of *museum*. She is a Research Affiliate at the Center for Arts and Cultural Policy Studies at Princeton, from which she received a project grant for her work on museums. Emily is currently employed at Balmori Associates in New York City and is a collaborator on an upcoming book by Agrest and Gandelsonas.

Alexander F. Briseño holds both a Bachelor of Architecture and a Master of Architecture from the University of Michigan and has also attended SCI-Arc. Alex has been a visiting professor at Pratt Institute and was awarded the 2003 Booth Fellowship from the University of Michigan for research on the palimpsestic nature of Italian cities. Alex is a senior designer at Perkins Eastman in New York City.

Jonathan D. Solomon holds a Bachelor of Arts in Urban Studies from Columbia University and a Master of Architecture from Princeton University, where he also earned a certificate in Media and Modernity. He teaches design at the City College of New York, and is the author of Pamphlet Architecture No. 26; *13 Projects for the Sheridan Expressway.* Jonathan currently works at Reiser+Umemoto in New York City.

Andrew Yang holds a Bachelor of Arts from the University of Chicago. He is an editor at *PRINT* magazine and contributes to *Surface*, *ARTnews* and *Frame*.